LEVEL 8 Supplemental

EXAM SERIES ANSWERS

By Glory St. Germain ARCT RMT MYCC UMTC &
Shelagh McKibbon-U'Ren RMT UMTC

ULTIMATE
MUSIC THEORY

GSG MUSIC

Enriching Lives Through Music Education

ISBN: 978-1-990358-18-0

The Ultimate Music Theory™ Program

Enriching Lives Through Music Education

The Ultimate Music Theory™ Workbooks & Answer Books Program includes:

UMT Rudiments Workbooks for Prep 1, Prep 2, Basic, Intermediate, Advanced & Complete
UMT Exam Series (Set #1 & Set #2) for Preparatory, Basic, Intermediate & Advanced

Supplemental Workbooks for PREP LEVEL, LEVELS 1 - 8 & COMPLETE LEVEL
UMT Supplemental Exam Series for LEVEL 5, LEVEL 6, LEVEL 7 & LEVEL 8

The Ultimate Music Theory Program is the *Way to Score Success* as UMT helps students prepare for nationally recognized theory examinations including the Royal Conservatory of Music.

Library and Archives Canada Cataloguing in Publication. UMT Workbooks & Exam Series /Glory St. Germain & Shelagh McKibbon-U'Ren. Respect Copyright. All rights reserved. GlorylandPublishing.com

Ultimate Music Theory Rudiments Exam Series

GP - EPS1	ISBN: 978-1-927641-00-2	Preparatory Rudiments Exams Set #1
GP - EPS1A	ISBN: 978-1-927641-08-8	Preparatory Exams Answers Set #1
GP - EPS2	ISBN: 978-1-927641-01-9	Preparatory Rudiments Exams Set #2
GP - EPS2A	ISBN: 978-1-927641-09-5	Preparatory Exams Answers Set #2
GP - EBS1	ISBN: 978-1-927641-02-6	Basic Rudiments Exams Set #1
GP - EBS1A	ISBN: 978-1-927641-10-1	Basic Exams Answers Set #1
GP - EBS2	ISBN: 978-1-927641-03-3	Basic Rudiments Exams Set #2
GP - EBS2A	ISBN: 978-1-927641-11-8	Basic Exams Answers Set #2
GP - EIS1	ISBN: 978-1-927641-04-0	Intermediate Rudiments Exams Set #1
GP - EIS1A	ISBN: 978-1-927641-12-5	Intermediate Exams Answers Set #1
GP - EIS2	ISBN: 978-1-927641-05-7	Intermediate Rudiments Exams Set #2
GP - EIS2A	ISBN: 978-1-927641-13-2	Intermediate Exams Answers Set #2
GP - EAS1	ISBN: 978-1-927641-06-4	Advanced Rudiments Exams Set #1
GP - EAS1A	ISBN: 978-1-927641-14-9	Advanced Exams Answers Set #1
GP - EAS2	ISBN: 978-1-927641-07-1	Advanced Rudiments Exams Set #2
GP - EAS2A	ISBN: 978-1-927641-15-6	Advanced Exams Answers Set #2

Ultimate Music Theory Supplemental Exam Series

GP-L5E	ISBN: 978-1-990358-11-1	LEVEL 5 Exams
GP-L5EA	ISBN: 978-1-990358-12-8	LEVEL 5 Exams Answers
GP-L6E	ISBN: 978-1-990358-13-5	LEVEL 6 Exams
GP-L6EA	ISBN: 978-1-990358-14-2	LEVEL 6 Exams Answers
GP-L7E	ISBN: 978-1-990358-15-9	LEVEL 7 Exams
GP-L7EA	ISBN: 978-1-990358-16-6	LEVEL 7 Exams Answers
GP-L8E	ISBN: 978-1-990358-17-3	LEVEL 8 Exams
GP-L8EA	ISBN: 978-1-990358-18-0	LEVEL 8 Exams Answers

Go to UltimateMusicTheory.com and check out the FREE Resources

Ultimate Music Theory FREE RESOURCES created just for you!

Ultimate Music Theory
LEVEL 8 Supplemental Exams

Table of Contents

LEVEL 8 MAP 4

LEVEL 8 Supplemental Exam #1 6

LEVEL 8 Supplemental Exam #2 9

LEVEL 8 Supplemental Exam #3 12

LEVEL 8 Supplemental Exam #4 15

LEVEL 8 Supplemental Exam #5 18

LEVEL 8 Supplemental Exam #6 21

LEVEL 8 Supplemental Exam #7 24

LEVEL 8 Supplemental Exam #8 27

LEVEL 8 Supplemental Bonus Exam 30

Ultimate Music Theory: *The Way to Score Success!*

The 2016 RCM Theory Syllabus **additional concepts** to the Level 8 (formerly Advanced Rudiments) Examination Requirements covered in the **UMT Supplemental LEVEL 8 Workbook** include:

♫ **Chords and Harmony**: Functional Chord Symbols and Root/Quality Chord Symbols for all Chords and Triads (in Root Position and inversions).
Identification and writing of Authentic, Half and Plagal Cadences on a Grand Staff in Keyboard Style and in Chorale Style.
Identification of Cluster Chords, Quartal Chords and Polychords.

♫ **Melody and Composition**: Melodic Passing Tones and Neighbor Tones (unaccented only) within a harmonic context of I, IV and V Chords (Major) and i, iv and V Chords (minor).
Composition of a Contrasting Period in a Major or minor key, given the first 2 measures.

♫ **Form and Analysis**: Identification of concepts from this and previous levels (in the 2016 Theory Syllabus) within short musical examples.
Application of Functional Chord Symbols (I, i, IV, iv, V, V7) and Root/Quality Chord Symbols (for example, C, Am, G7) for the implied harmonies of a melody using root position & inversions, maintaining a clearly defined harmonic rhythm.
Identification of Types of Motion: Parallel, Similar, Contrary, Oblique and Static.

♫ **Musical Terms and Signs**: New Terms and Signs have been added.

♫ **Music History**: Expanding Musical Horizons: Ordo Virtutum (Hildegard von Bingen); Sumer Is Icumen In, "Reading Rota" (Anonymous); El grillo (Josquin des Prez); "Kaboran (Gamelan Prawa)"; "Evening Raga: Bhopali".

Study and Memorize the UMT Map - LEVEL 8

Circle of Fifths

♭B E A D G C F   ♯F C G D A E B

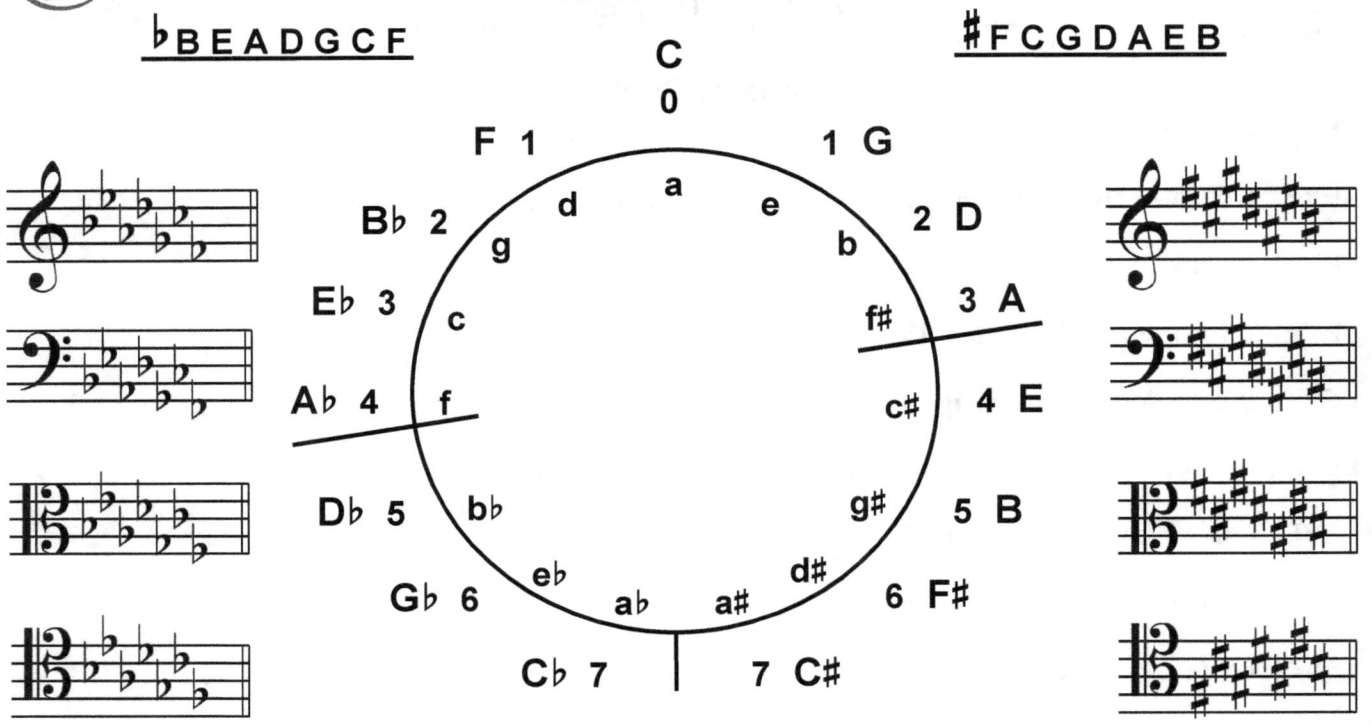

Chorale Vocal Range:

Soprano: Alto: Tenor: Bass:

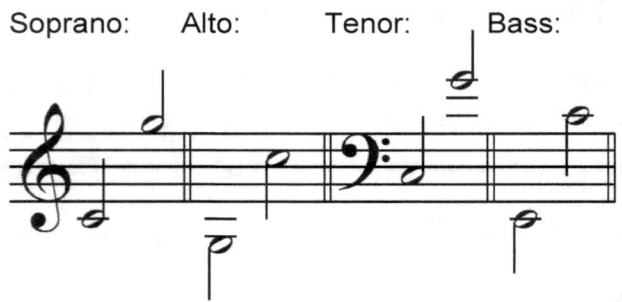

Scores:

Modern Vocal: String Quartet:

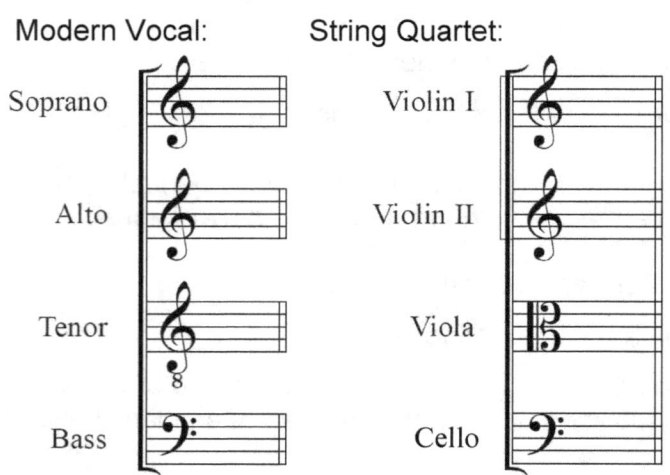

	Modern Vocal	String Quartet
Soprano		Violin I
Alto		Violin II
Tenor		Viola
Bass		Cello

Cadences	Major	minor
Authentic: (Perfect)	V - I, V7 - I	V - i, V7 - i
Plagal:	IV - I	iv - i
Half: (Imperfect)	I - V or IV - V*	i - V or iv - V*

(*no common note, voices descend)

Melody Writing   Parallel Period: a + a1

Contrary Period: a + b

Scale Degrees   Stable: $\hat{1}$ and $\hat{3}$

Unstable: $\hat{7}$ and $\hat{2}$

V7 - I Cadence   Complete V7 to Incomplete I (i)
or
Incomplete V7 to Complete I (i)

Tritone Tendency Tones $\hat{7}$ to $\hat{1}$ and $\hat{4}$ to $\hat{3}$

Circle of Fifths

♭BEADGCF   C   #FCGDAEB

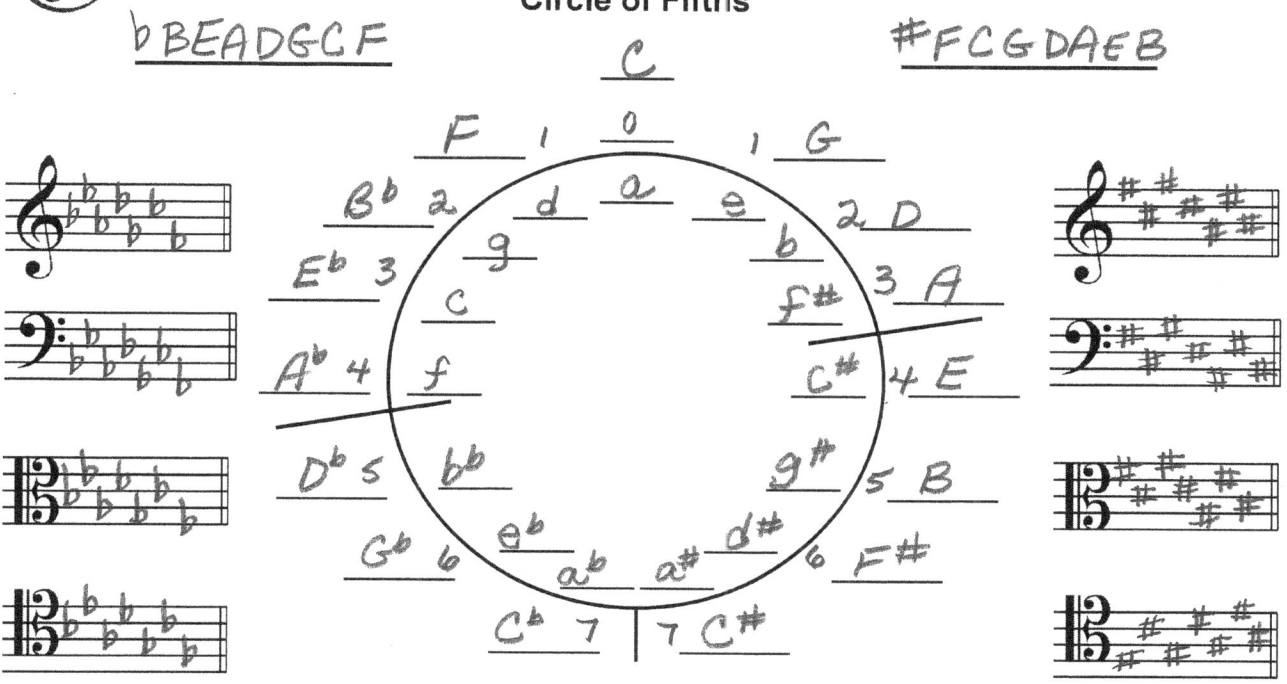

Chorale Vocal Range:

Soprano : Alto : Tenor : Bass

Scores:

Modern Vocal: String Quartet:

Soprano   Violin I

Alto   Violin II

Tenor   Viola

Bass   Cello

Cadences

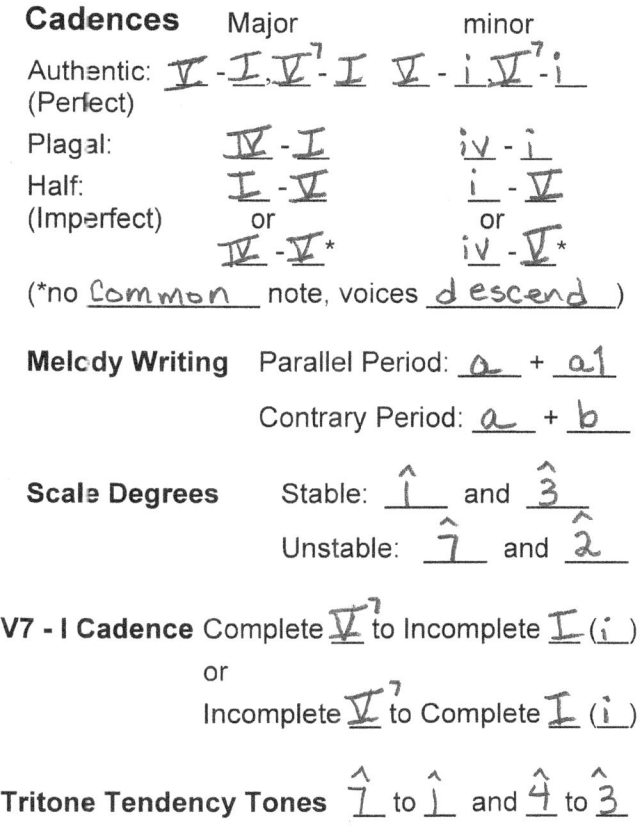

	Major	minor
Authentic: (Perfect)	V - I, V^7 - I	V - i, V^7 - i
Plagal:	IV - I	iv - i
Half: (Imperfect)	I - V	i - V
	or	or
	IV - V*	iv - V*

(*no Common note, voices descend)

Melody Writing   Parallel Period: a + a1

Contrary Period: a + b

Scale Degrees   Stable: $\hat{1}$ and $\hat{3}$

Unstable: $\hat{7}$ and $\hat{2}$

V7 - I Cadence Complete V^7 to Incomplete I (i)

or

Incomplete V^7 to Complete I (i)

Tritone Tendency Tones $\hat{7}$ to $\hat{1}$ and $\hat{4}$ to $\hat{3}$

Ultimate Music Theory
LEVEL 8 Supplemental Exam #1

Total Score: ____
50

Use with Advanced Exam Set #1 - Exam #1

The Ultimate Music Theory™ Advanced Rudiments Workbook, LEVELS 7 & 8 Supplemental Workbooks, Advanced Rudiments Exam Series and LEVEL 8 Supplemental Exams prepare students for successful completion of the Royal Conservatory of Music Level 8 Theory Examination.

1. a) Write the following Seventh Chords. Use accidentals. Use half notes.

Root/Quality
Chord Symbol: D7/A   E7/G♯   F°7   C♭7   B♯°7   A7/C♯

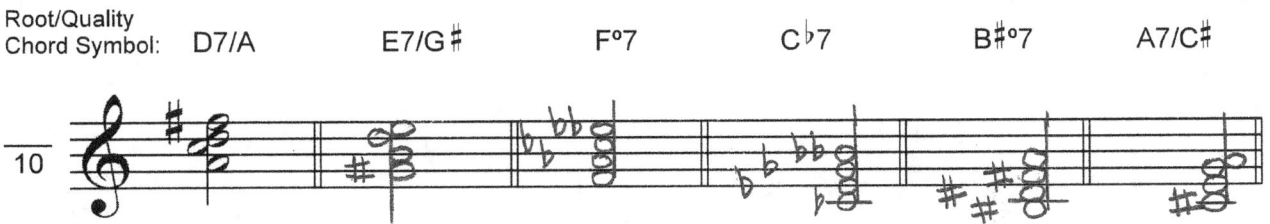

b) Write the following Triads in B Major. Use accidentals. Use half notes.

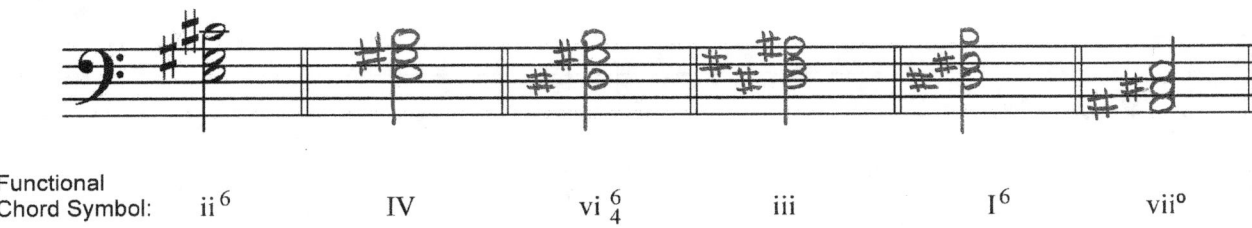

Functional
Chord Symbol: ii^6 IV   vi$^6_4$ iii   I^6 vii°

2.   For each of the following Triads and Seventh Chords:

a) Name the minor key.
b) Write the Functional Chord Symbol below the staff.

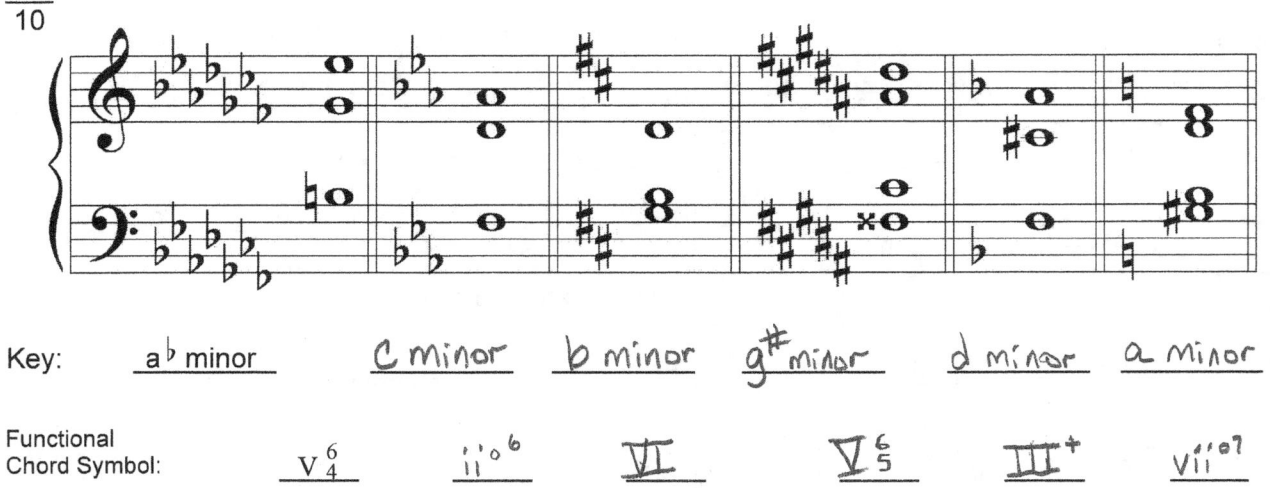

Key: a♭ minor   C minor   b minor   g♯ minor   d minor   a minor

Functional
Chord Symbol: V$^6_4$ ii°^{6} VI   V$^6_5$ III$^+$ vii°7

3. For the following Melodic Opening:

   a) Name the key of the melody.
   b) Write the Time Signature directly on the music.
   __10__ c) Continue the given melody to create a Question Phrase. End on an unstable scale degree.
   d) Compose an Answer Phrase to create a Contrasting Period. End on a stable scale degree. (There will be more than one correct answer.)
   e) Draw a phrase mark (slur) over each phrase.
   f) Name the type of each cadence (Authentic or Half) at the end of each phrase.

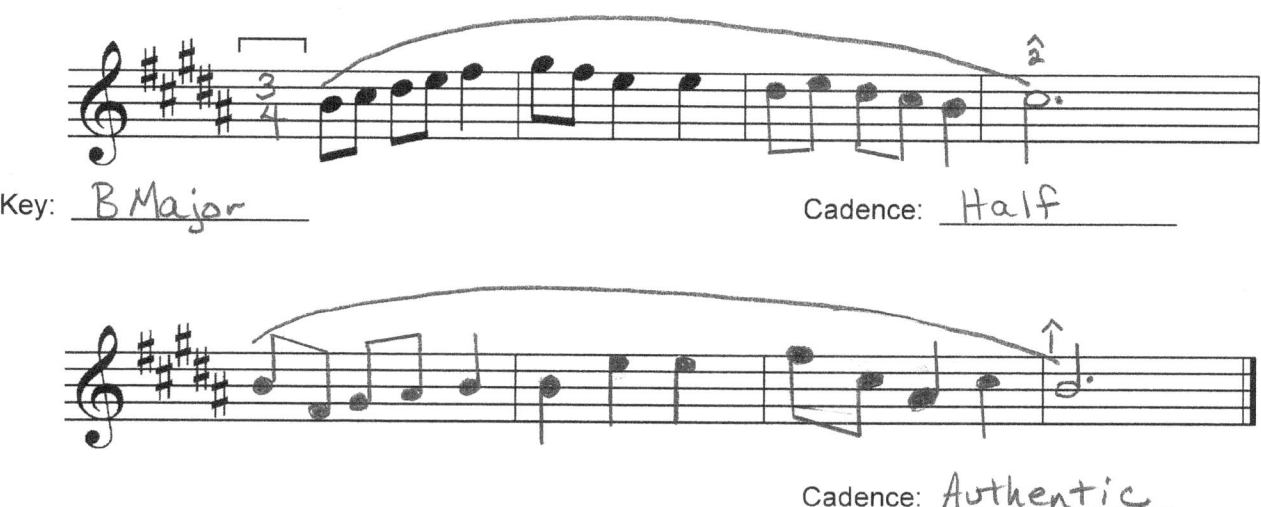

Key: B Major   Cadence: Half

Cadence: Authentic

4. For each of the following Cadences:

   a) Name the key.
   b) Identify the type of Cadence (Authentic, Half or Plagal) and the chords used.
   c) Identify the style as Keyboard or Chorale.

__10__

Key:	g minor	A Major	e minor	b♭ minor
Type:	Plagal (iv - i)	Half (IV-V)	Half (i-V)	Authentic (V-i)
Style:	Chorale	Keyboard	Chorale	Keyboard

Ultimate Music Theory
LEVEL 8 Supplemental Exam #1

5. Answer any 10 (Ten) of the following. (All answers are given. On the exam, provide answers for only 10.)

a) Name the Composer of "El grillo".

10 _____ Josquin des Prez

b) Name the Composer of "Ordo Virtutum".

Hildegard von Bingen

c) Name the Genre of "Sumer Is Icumen In".

Perpetual Round (Imitative Canon)

d) Name the Genre of "Ordo Virtutum".

Morality Play (Plainchant)

e) Name the Type of Ensemble featuring gongs, xylophones, metallophones, drums and voices.

Gamelan

f) Name the plucked Indian Instrument with moveable frets and multiple strings.

Sitar

g) Name an expressive device used in "El grillo" to depict the text.

Word Painting

h) Name the Texture of "Sumer Is Icumen In".

Polyphonic texture

i) Name the Texture of "Ordo Virtutum".

Monophonic texture

j) Name the Period or Era when "El grillo" was written.

Renaissance Era (ca 1450 - ca 1600)

k) Name the Period or Era when "Sumer Is Icumen In" was written.

13th Century - Medieval Era

l) Name the Period or Era when "Ordo Virtutum" was written.

Middle Ages - Medieval Era (ca 476 - 1450)

1. Add the correct Time Signature below the bracket for each of the following rhythms.

2. Write the following Seventh Chords. Use whole notes. Use accidentals.

3. a) For each of the following triads:
    i. Name the minor key.
    ii. Write the Functional Chord Symbol below the staff.

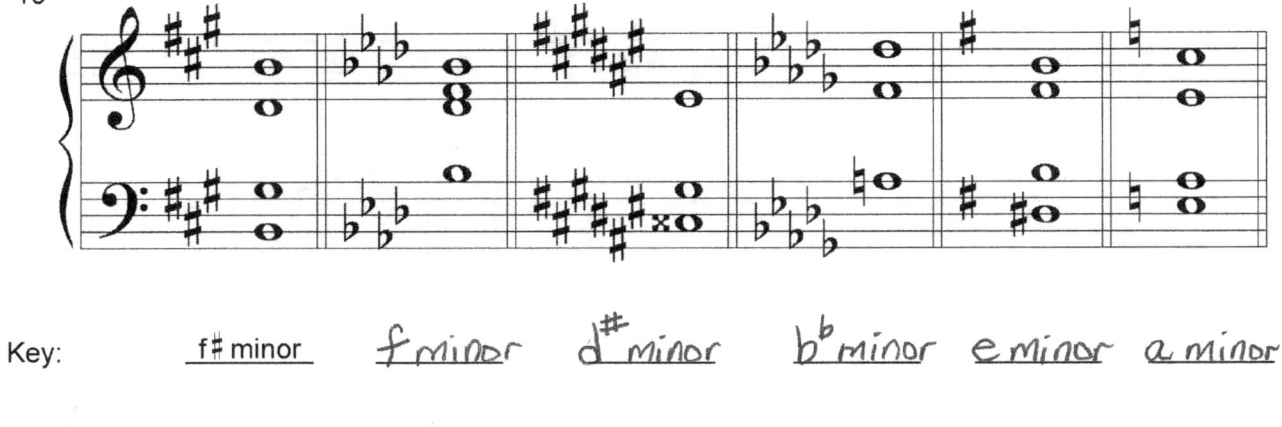

Key: f♯ minor   f minor   d♯ minor   b♭ minor   e minor   a minor

Functional Chord Symbol: ii°⁶   iv   vii°   III⁺⁶₄   V⁶   i⁶₄

(or ii°⁶₃)

b) For each of the following triads:
    i. Name the Major key.
    ii. Write the Root/Quality Chord Symbol above the staff.

Root/Quality Chord Symbol: G♯°/B   D♭/A♭   D♯m   D♭/F   D   Em

(or G♯dim/B)

Key: A Major   A♭ Major   F♯ Major   D♭ Major   G Major   C Major

4. a) Name the key of the following melody.
    b) In the given melody, write the Functional Chord Symbols on the lines below each measure.
    c) In the given melody, circle any Passing Tones. Label them as "pt".
    d) In the given melody, circle any Neighbor Tones. Label them as "nt".
    10 e) Rewrite the melody at the same pitch. Use a Key Signature and any necessary accidentals.

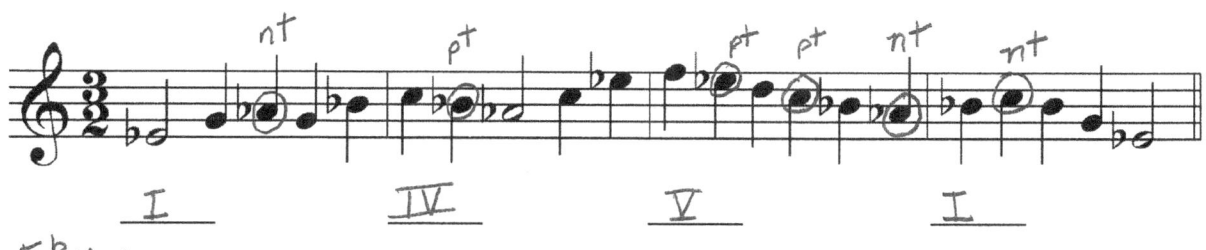

Key: E♭ Major

5. Match each musical term or sign with the English definition. (Not all definitions will be used.)

Term		Definition	
tranquillo	c	a)	two octaves higher
con sordino	e	b)	fast
tutti	h	c)	quiet, tranquil
grandioso	f	d)	becoming faster, pressing
mit Ausdruck	l	e)	with mute
quindicesima alta	a	f)	grandly
stringendo	d	g)	moderately, moderate
attaca	k	h)	a passage for the ensemble
langsam	j	i)	at the same tempo
schnell	b	j)	slowly, slow
massig, mässig, mäßig (Any version may be used)	g	k)	proceed without a break
		l)	with expression

10

1.   For the following Melodic Opening:

   a) Name the key of the melody.
   b) Write the Time Signature below the bracket.
__10__ c) Complete the first phrase. End on an unstable scale degree. Name the type of cadence.
      (There will be more than one correct answer.)
   d) Compose an Answer Phrase to create a Contrary Period. End on a stable scale degree.
      Name the type of cadence. (There will be more than one correct answer.)
   e) Draw a phrase mark (slur) over each phrase.

Key: __A♭ Major__   Cadence: __Half__

Cadence: __Authentic__

2.   Write the following Close Position Solid (Blocked) Triads and Chords. Use whole notes.
      Use a Key Signature and any necessary accidentals. Write the Root/Quality Chord Symbol
      above and the Functional Chord Symbol below.

__10__ a) The Submediant Triad of a minor harmonic, in first inversion.
      b) The Dominant Seventh Chord of C Major, in third inversion.
      c) The Mediant Triad of g minor harmonic, in second inversion.
      d) The Diminished Seventh Chord of c sharp minor harmonic, in root position.
      e) The Supertonic Triad of D flat Major, in root position.

Root/Quality
Chord Symbol: a) __F/A__   b) __G⁷/F__   c) __B♭⁺/F♯__   d) __B♯°⁷__   e) __E♭m__

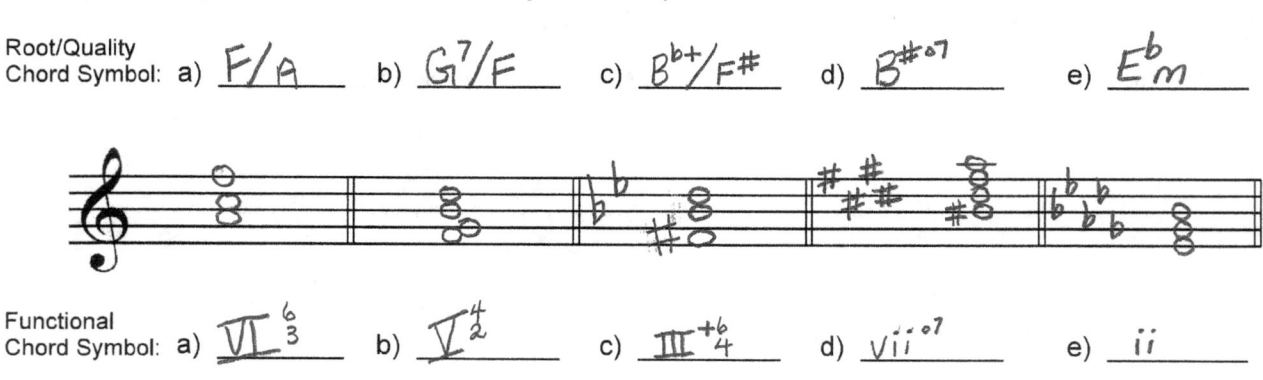

Functional
Chord Symbol: a) __VI⁶₃__   b) __V⁴₂__   c) __III⁺⁶₄__   d) __vii°⁷__   e) __ii__

3. Add Bar Lines to complete the following rhythms.

10

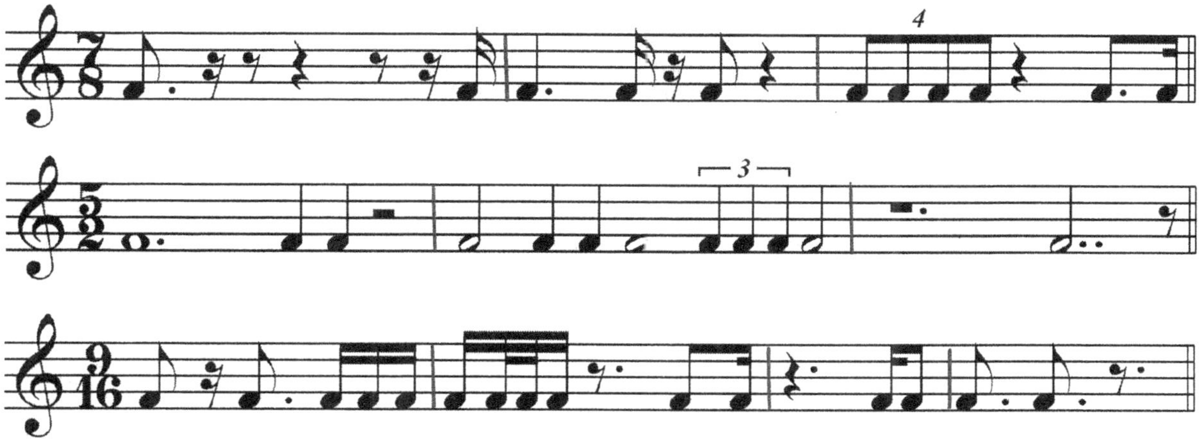

4. Write the term or word for each statement. Use the following terms or words. (Not all terms or words will be used.)

Morality Play   Plainchant   Ordo Virtutum   Canon   Word Painting   Drone

10

Tala   Sitar   Stringendo   Allargando   Renaissance   Raga   Medieval

a) <u>Word Painting</u> - The technique of writing music that used melody, rhythm and/or harmony to reflect the meaning of the text.

b) <u>Ordo Virtutum</u> - A Medieval liturgical drama composed around the year 1151 by Hildegard of Bingen.

c) <u>Sitar</u> - A multi-stringed instrument with moveable frets, a hollow neck and a gourd-shaped resonance chamber.

d) <u>Morality Play</u> - The genre of a medieval drama and music that used allegorical or symbolic figures to teach a religious idea.

e) <u>Raga</u> - Meaning "color, passion or emotion", the melodic structure is based on a pattern of pitches and intervals.

f) <u>Tala</u> - Meaning "clap", a musical meter that repeats in a rhythmic cycle from the beginning to the end of the music.

g) <u>Canon</u> - A simple round sung by 2 or more voices where, when each voice finished, it starts again at the beginning.

h) <u>Plain chant</u> - A modal melody in free rhythm, with a monophonic texture, used with Latin texts in the liturgies.

i) <u>Stringendo</u> - A tempo mark that indicates pressing, to press ahead, becoming faster.

j) <u>Allargando</u> - A tempo mark that indicates to become slower, broadening.

5. This excerpt is taken from Ultimate Music Theory Student Olivia Allen's composition entitled "Sonatina in C Major". Analyze this excerpt by answering the questions below.

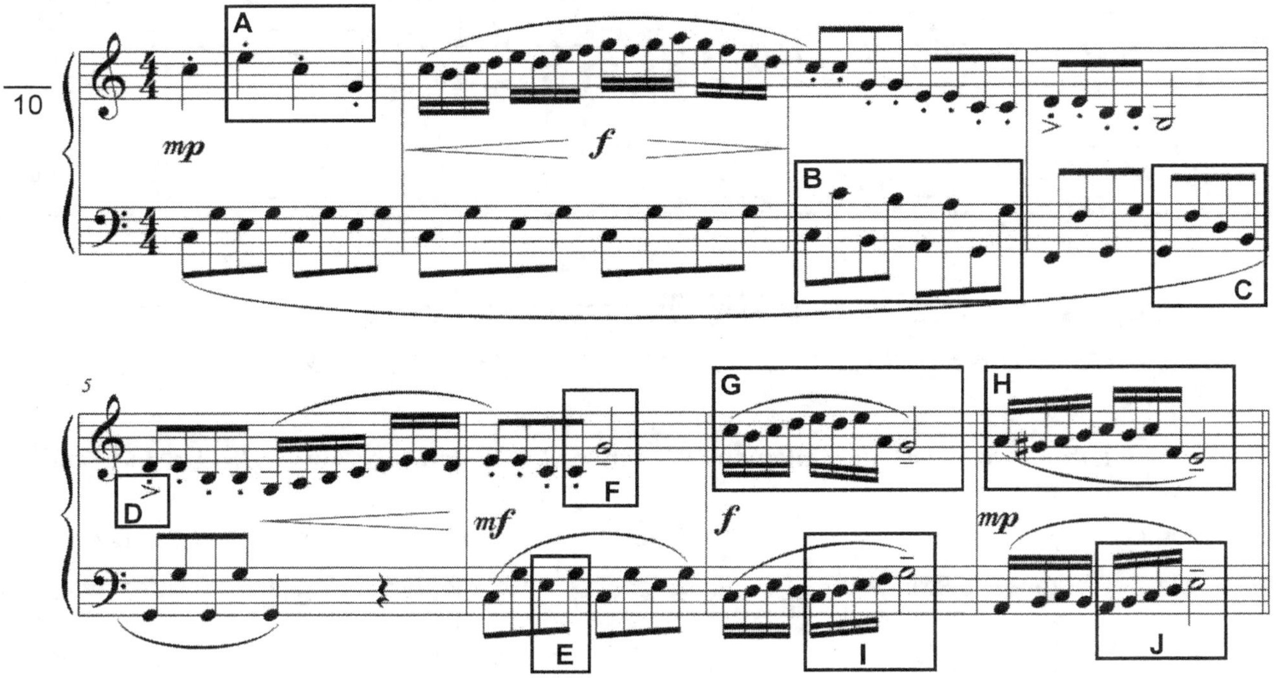

a) For the triad at **A**, identify: Root: __C__ ; Quality: __Major__ ; Position: __2nd inv__ .

b) Identify the intervals at **B** as an example of: ☐ Parallel Fifths or ☑ Parallel Eighths

c) For the chord at **C**, identify: Root: __G__ ; Quality: __Dom 7th__ ; Position: __Root pos__

d) Name the signs at **D**: __Staccato and accent__

e) Identify the interval at **E**: __min 3__ . Identify the interval at **F**: __Per 5__ .

f) Identify the relationship of the notes at **G** and **H** as: ☑ Transposition or ☐ Inversion.

g) For the Pentascale at **I**, identify: Root: __C__ ; Quality: __Major__ .

h) For the Pentascale at **J**, identify: Root: __A__ ; Quality: __minor__ .

i) In this excerpt, identify the number of Tenuto Marks (Tenuto Signs): __5__ .

j) In this excerpt, identify the number of Slurs (Phrases): __8__ ; Ties: __0__ .

1. For each of the following melodic examples:

   i) Name the Key Signature.
   ii) Add the Time Signature directly on the staff.
   iii) Identify the Type of Melodic Motion between the two voices as Parallel, Similar, Contrary, Oblique or Static.

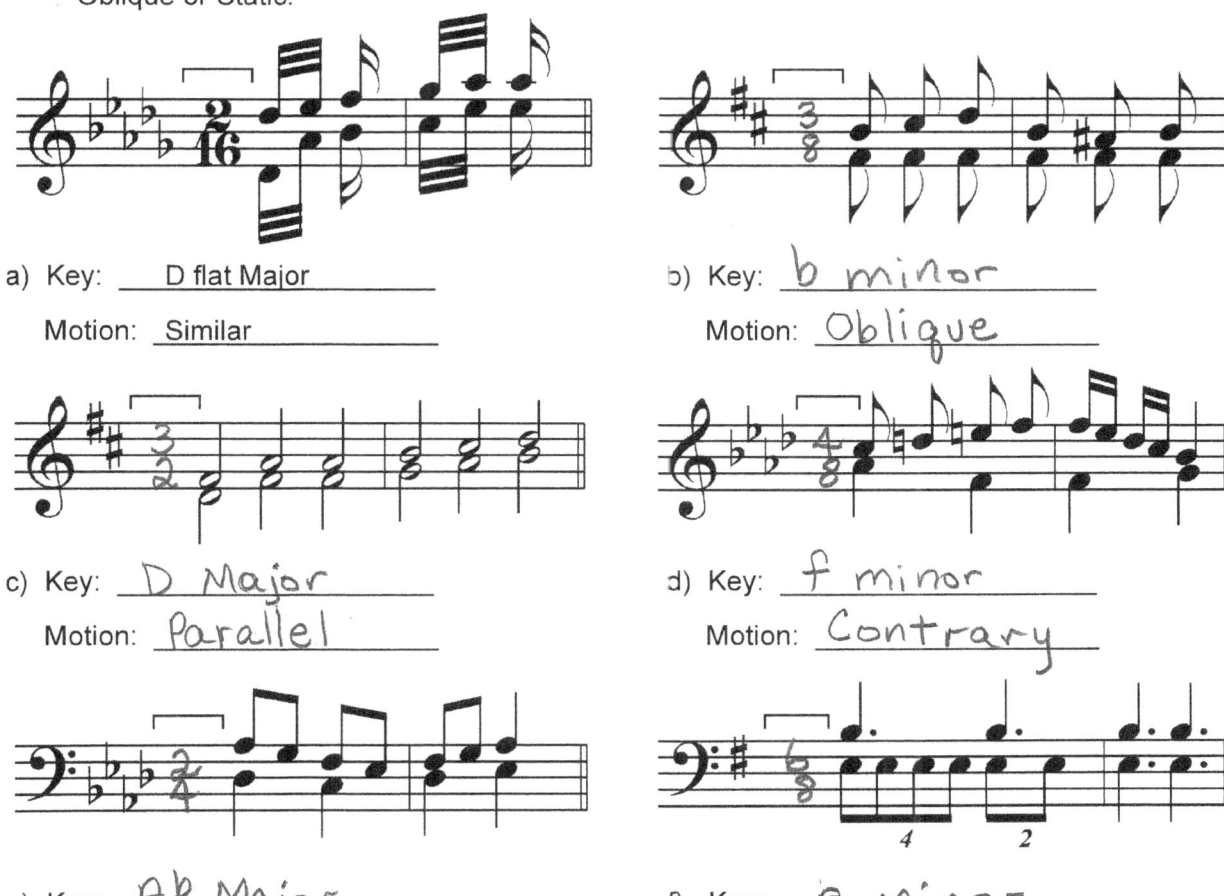

a) Key: ___D flat Major___

   Motion: ___Similar___

b) Key: ___b minor___

   Motion: ___Oblique___

c) Key: ___D Major___

   Motion: ___Parallel___

d) Key: ___f minor___

   Motion: ___Contrary___

e) Key: ___Ab Major___

   Motion: ___Similar___

f) Key: ___e minor___

   Motion: ___Static___

2. Write the melodic interval below the given note. Use whole notes.

10

   a) diminished 10   b) Augmented 5   c) Major 14   d) Perfect 11   e) diminished 15

3. For the following Melodic Opening:

   a) Name the key of the melody.
   b) Complete the first phrase. End on an unstable scale degree. Name the type of cadence.
   (There will be more than one correct answer.)
   c) Compose an Answer Phrase to create a Contrary Period. End on a stable scale degree. Name the type of cadence. (There will be more than one correct answer.)
   d) Draw a phrase mark (slur) over each phrase.

__10__

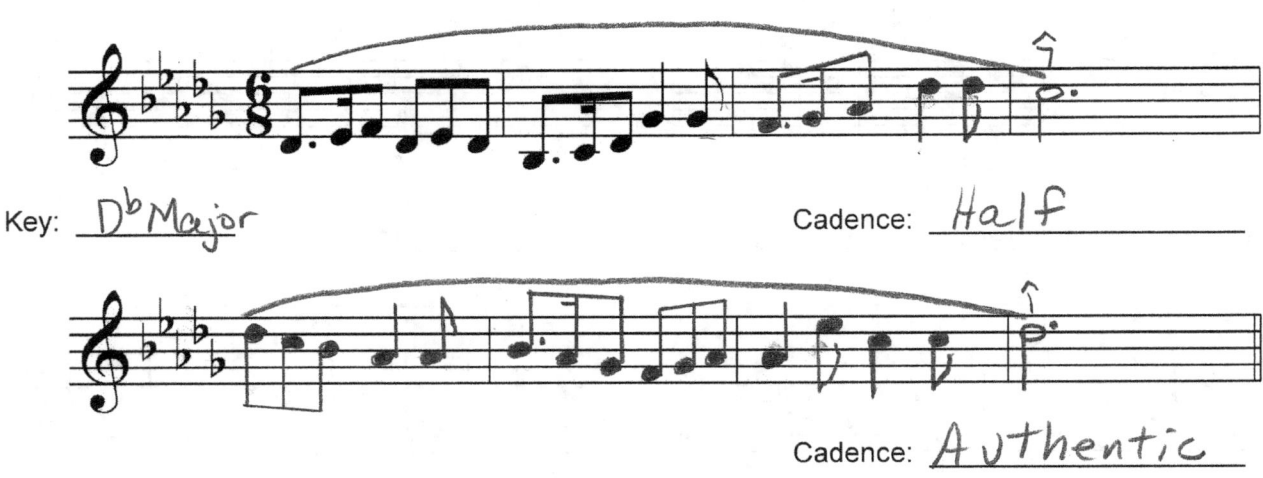

Key: Db Major   Cadence: Half

Cadence: Authentic

4. Circle TRUE or FALSE for each of the following statements.

   a) TRUE or (FALSE) Hildegard von Bingen's *Ordo Virtutum* uses Polyphonic Texture.

__10__ b) TRUE or (FALSE) *Sumer Is Icumen In* uses Monophonic Texture.

   c) (TRUE) or FALSE: *El grillo* uses Word Painting to connect the text with the music.

   d) TRUE or (FALSE) An *ostinato* is a melodic or rhythmic pattern that is heard only once.

   e) (TRUE) or FALSE: A Morality Play is a Medieval genre that combines music and drama.

   f) TRUE or (FALSE) Cluster Chords combine 2 or more different chords to create dissonance.

   g) (TRUE) or FALSE: A Gamelan is a traditional Javanese instrumental ensemble.

   h) (TRUE) or FALSE: Meaning "to clap", *tala* provides rhythmic structure in Indian Music.

   i) TRUE or (FALSE) Meaning "color", a *raga* is a 5-stringed plucked instrument with frets.

   j) (TRUE) or FALSE: A *frottola* is a secular polyphonic 15th Century Italian vocal genre.

5. Analyze this excerpt from Olivia Allen's Sonatina in C Major by answering the questions below.

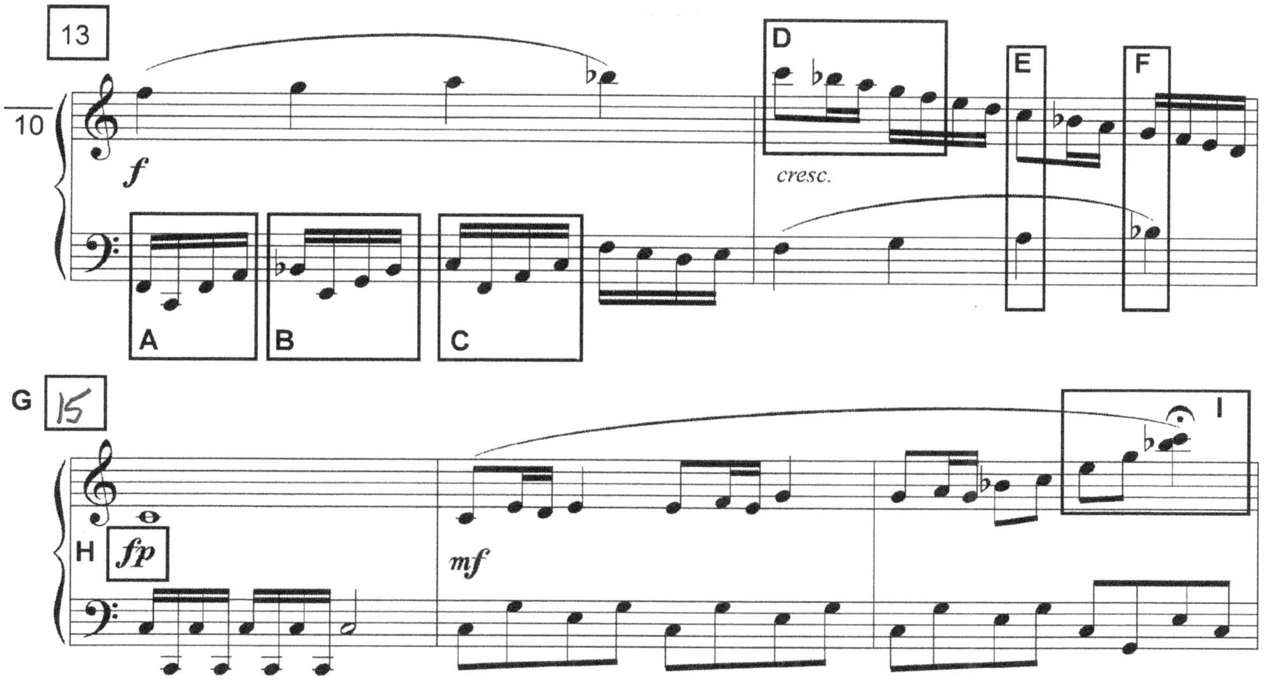

a) In this excerpt, an accidental has been added. What Key is formed as a result? *F Major*

b) For the triad at **A**, identify: Root: *F* ; Quality: *Major* ; Position: *2nd inv*.

c) For the triad at **B**, identify: Root: *E* ; Quality: *dim* ; Position: *Root pos*.

d) For the triad at **C**, identify: Root: *F* ; Quality: *Major* ; Position: *Root pos*.

e) For the Pentascale at **D**, identify: Direction: *descending* Quality: *Major*.

f) For the Interval at **E**, name the notes: *A* *C* . Name the interval: *min 10*.

g) For the Interval at **F**, name the notes: *B♭* *G* . Name the interval: *Maj 6*.

h) This excerpt begins on Measure 13. Add the correct Measure Number at **G**.

i) Explain the Dynamic Sign at **H**. *fortepiano – loud, suddenly soft*

j) For the chord at **I**, identify: Type: *Dominant 7th* ; Position: *1st inv*.

1.   a) Write the following harmonic intervals below each of the given notes.

10

       Major 10   Augmented 5   diminished 8   minor 13   Perfect 4

b) Invert the above intervals in the Alto Clef. Name the inversions.

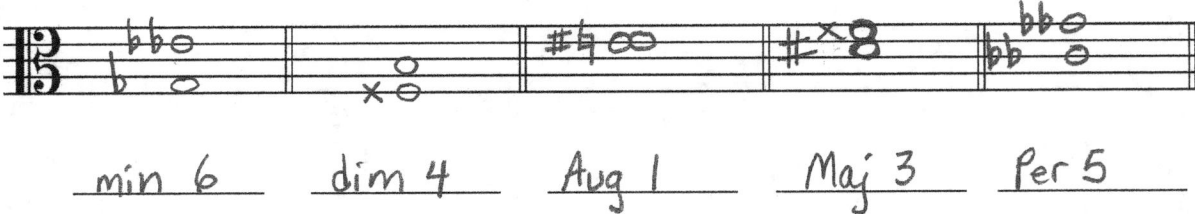

   min 6   dim 4   Aug 1   Maj 3   Per 5

2.   For the following Melodic Opening:

    a) Name the key of the melody.
____ b) Continue the given melodic opening to create a Question Phrase. End on an unstable scale
10   degree. (There will be more than one correct answer.)
    c) Compose an Answer Phrase to create a Contrasting Period. End on a stable scale degree.
       (There will be more than one correct answer.)
    d) Draw a phrase mark (slur) over each phrase.
    e) Name the type of each Cadence as Authentic or Half.

Key: _d minor_   Cadence: _Half_

                                    Cadence: _Authentic_

3. For each of the following triads or chords:

    a) Name the minor key.

____ b) Write the Root/Quality Chord Symbol above each Triad or Chord.

10 c) Write the Functional Chord Symbol below each Triad or Chord.

Root/Quality
Chord Symbol: F°/C♭   A#°7   A♭+/C   C#m/G#   A7/E

Key: e♭ minor   b minor   f minor   g# minor   d minor

Functional
Chord Symbol: $ii°^6_4$ $vii°^7$ III^{+6} iv^6_4 V^4_3

4. Write the following triads or chords in Close Position. Use a Key Signature and accidentals if needed. Use whole notes.

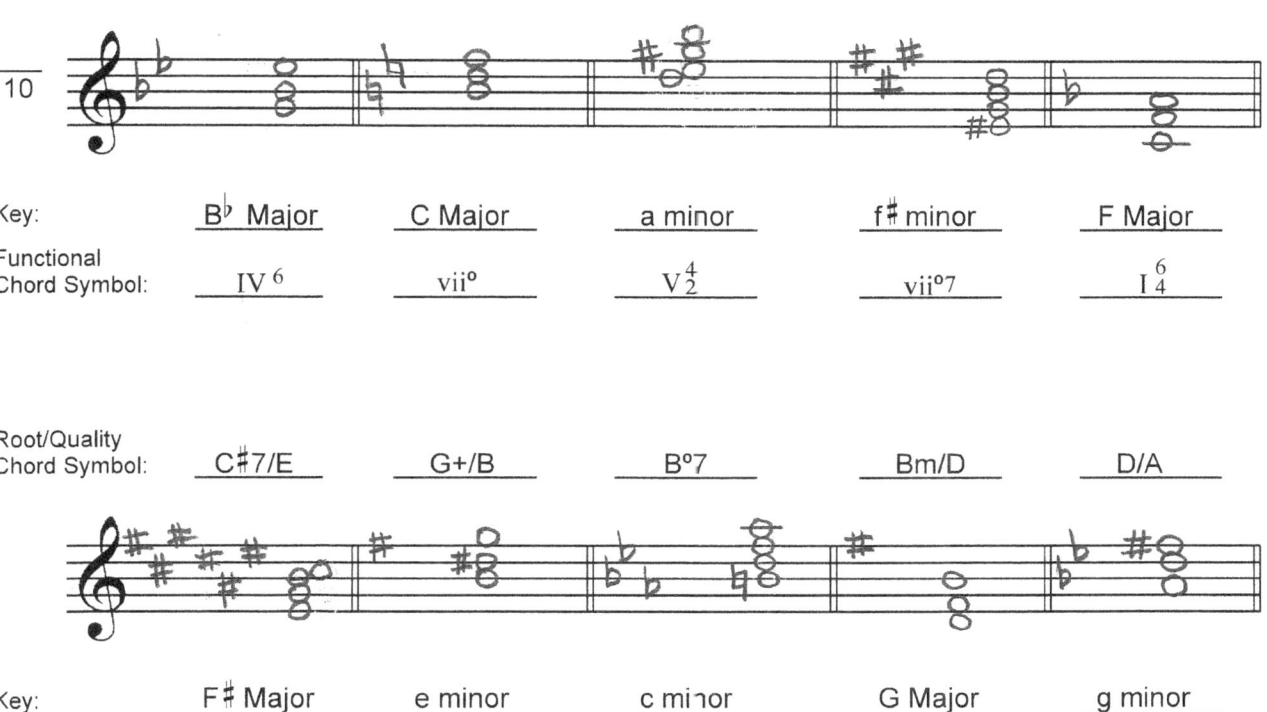

Key: B♭ Major   C Major   a minor   f# minor   F Major

Functional
Chord Symbol: IV^6 $vii°$ V^4_2 $vii°7$ I^6_4

Root/Quality
Chord Symbol: C#7/E   G+/B   B°7   Bm/D   D/A

Key: F# Major   e minor   c minor   G Major   g minor

5. Analyze this excerpt from Olivia Allen's Sonatina in C Major by answering the questions below.

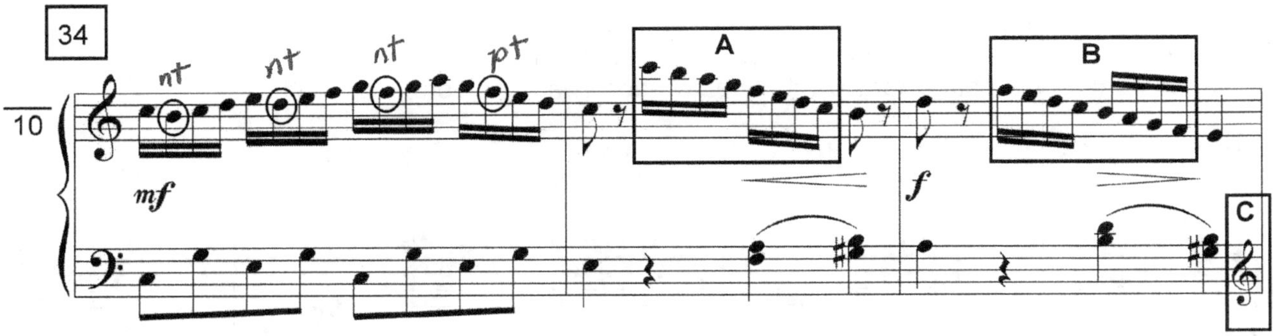

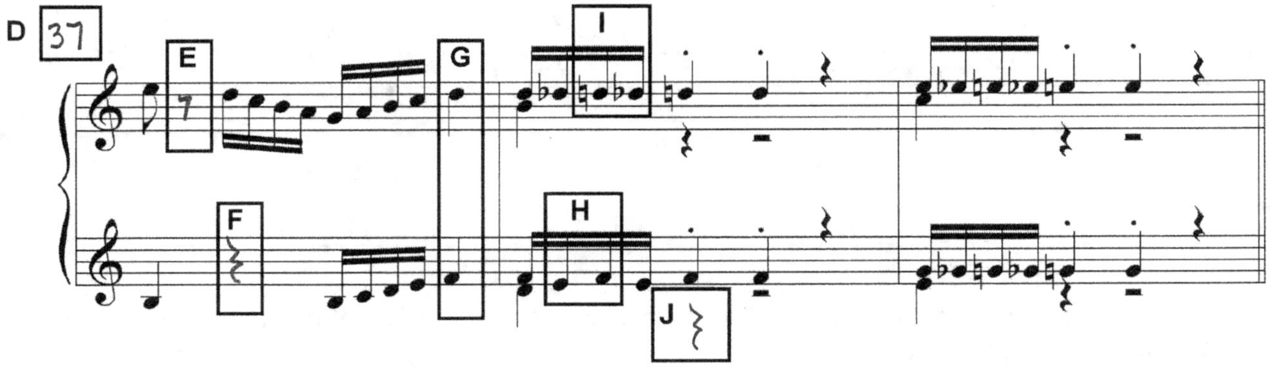

a) In M. 34, identify each circled note on the music as pt (passing tone) or nt (neighbour tone).

b) Identify the Modes at **A**: _Ionian_ ; **B**: _Lydian_ .

c) Explain the sign at **C**. _change to Treble Clef (left hand)_

d) This excerpt begins on Measure 34. Add the correct Measure Number at **D**.

e) Identify and add the correct rest at **E**: _eighth rest_ ; **F**: _quarter rest_ .

f) For the Interval at **G**, name the notes: _F D_ . Name the interval: _Maj 6_ .

g) Identify the distances as WS (whole step) or HS (half step) at **H**: _HS_ ; **I**: _HS_ .

h) Identify the Texture in the final 2 measures as: ☐ Monophonic or ☑ Polyphonic.

i) Add the correct rest at **J**. Explain why this rest is written below the staff: _The quarter_
rest is written below the staff as it is the Bass voice

1. Write the following Chords and Triads in Close Position. Use whole notes. Observe the Key Signature and use any accidentals as necessary.

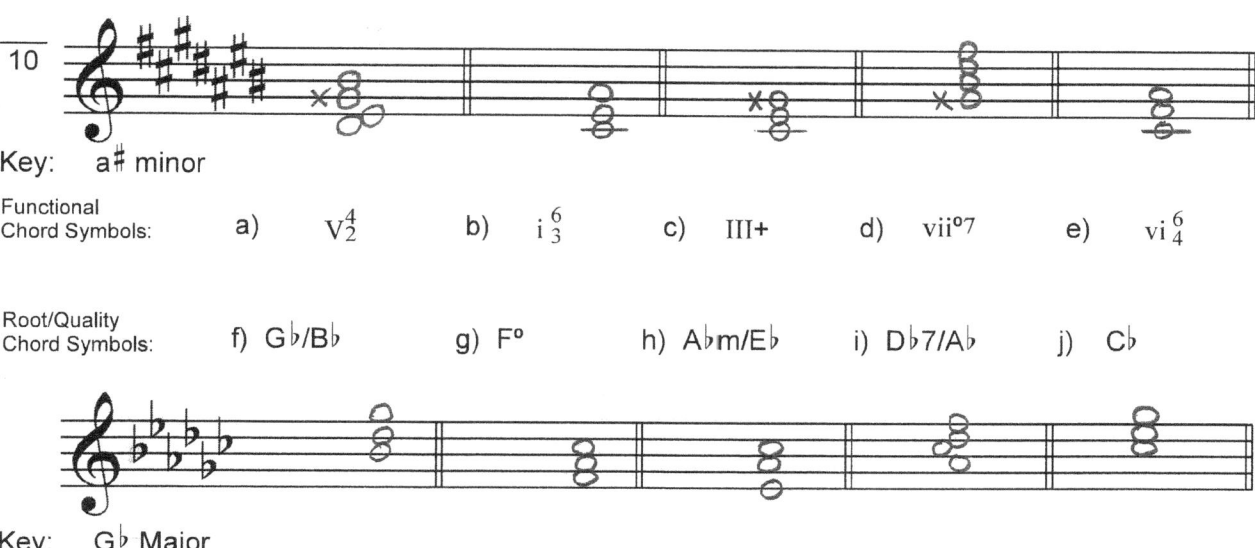

Key: a# minor

Functional Chord Symbols: a) V_2^4 b) i_3^6 c) III+   d) vii°7   e) vi_4^6

Root/Quality Chord Symbols: f) G♭/B♭   g) F°   h) A♭m/E♭   i) D♭7/A♭   j) C♭

Key: G♭ Major

2. For the following Melodic Opening:

   a) Name the key of the melody.

   b) Continue the given melodic opening to create a Question Phrase. End on an unstable scale degree. (There will be more than one correct answer.)

   c) Compose an Answer Phrase to create a Contrasting Period. End on a stable scale degree. (There will be more than one correct answer.)

   d) Draw a phrase mark (slur) over each phrase.

   e) Name the type of each Cadence as Authentic or Half.

Key: E♭ Major   Cadence: Half

Cadence: Authentic

3. Explain the meaning of the following terms.

    a) *comodo con espressione*: at a comfortable, easy tempo with expression

    b) *mesto ed ritenuto*: sad, mournful and suddenly slower, held back .

    ___
    10

    c) *pizzicato*: pluck the strings (for stringed instruments) .

    d) *sotto voce*: soft, subdued, under the breath .

    e) *agitato e vivo*: agitated and lively .

4. Identify the work to which each of the following statements applies by writing the appropriate letter (A, B or C) in the space before each statement.

    A - Ordo Virtutum
    B - Sumer Is Icumen In
    ___ C - El grillo
    10

    a) __B__ This work is also known as a "Reading Rota".

    b) __A__ This work is written in Monophonic Texture.

    c) __A__ This Genre of this work is a morality play.

    d) __C__ The Genre of this work is a frottola.

    e) __B__ This Genre of this work is a vocal work in the form of a round.

    f) __C__ This work is based on playful poems and uses word painting.

    g) __B__ This work features ostinato in the two bottom voices.

    h) __A__ This work features Latin text and unmeasured rhythm.

    i) __C__ The English translation of this work is "the cricket".

    j) __A__ This work was written by Hildegard von Bingen.

5. Analyze this excerpt from Olivia Allen's Sonatina in C Major by answering the questions below.

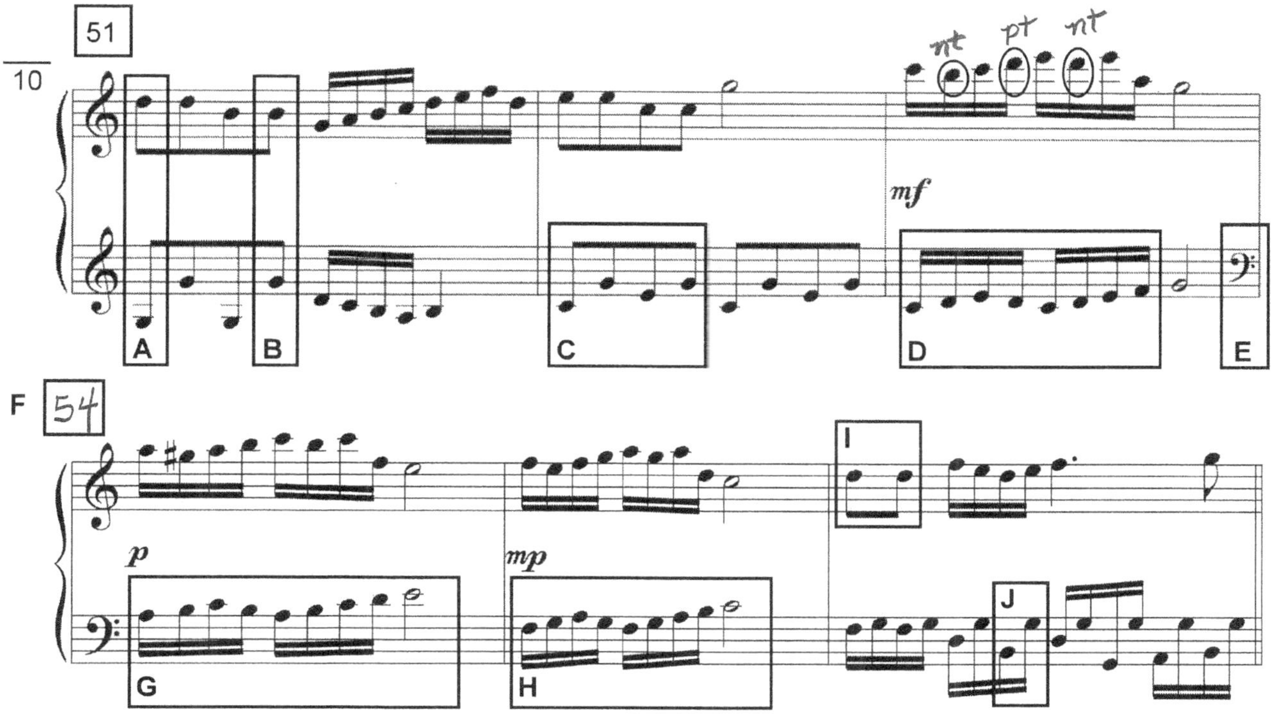

a) For the Interval at **A**, name the notes: __G__ __D__ . Name the interval: __Per 12__ .

b) For the Interval at **B**, name the notes: __G__ __B__ . Name the interval: __Maj 3__ .

c) For the Triad at **C**, identify: Root: __C__ Quality: __Major__ Position: __Root pos__ .

d) In M. 53, identify each circled note on the music as pt (passing tone) or nt (neighbour tone).

e) Circle to identify the movement of the notes at **D** as: (Conjunct) or Disjunct.

f) Explain the sign at **E**: __change to Bass Clef (left hand)__ .

g) This excerpt begins on Measure 51. Add the measure number at **F**.

h) Circle the relationship of the melodic pattern at **G** and **H** as: (Transposition) or Inversion.

i) For the Interval at **I**, name the notes: __D__ __D__ . Name the interval: __Per 1__ .

j) For the Interval at **J**, name the notes: __B__ __G__ . Name the interval: __min 6__ .

Ultimate Music Theory
LEVEL 8 Supplemental Exam #7

Total Score: ____ / 50

Use with Advanced Exam Set 2 - Exam #3

1. a) Write the Root/Quality Chord Symbols above the following Triads and Chords.

____ / 10

Root/Quality Chord Symbols: a) A#m/C# b) C# c) G#7/D# d) F#/C# e) B#°/D#

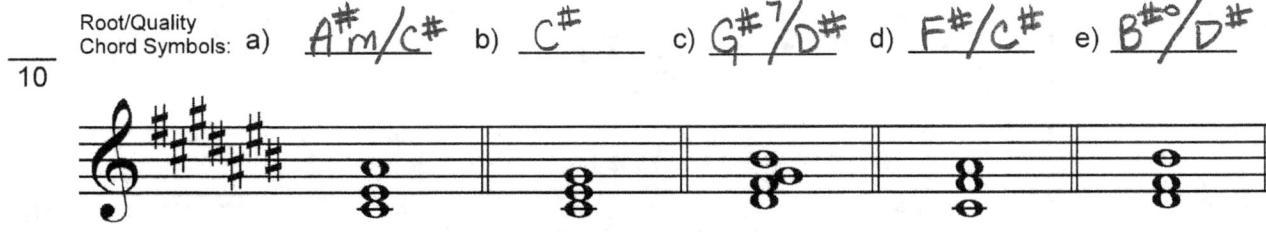

Key: C# Major

b) Write the Functional Chord Symbols below the following Triads and Chords.

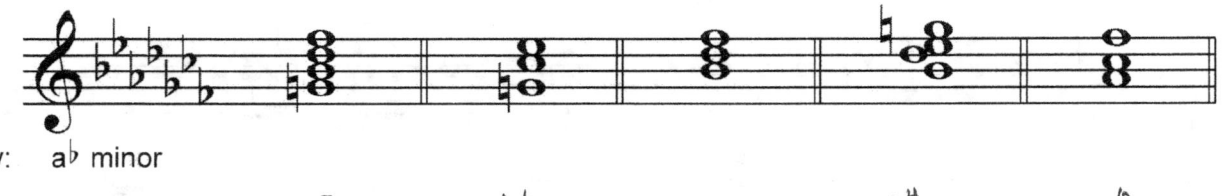

Key: ab minor

Functional Chord Symbols: f) vii°7 g) III+6/4 h) ii° i) V4/3 j) VI6

2. For the following Melodic Opening:

a) Name the key of the melody.

____ / 10 b) Continue the given melodic opening to create a Question Phrase. End on an unstable scale degree. (There will be more than one correct answer.)

c) Compose an Answer Phrase to create a Contrasting Period. End on a stable scale degree. (There will be more than one correct answer.)

d) Draw a phrase mark (slur) over each phrase.

e) Name the type of each Cadence as Authentic or Half.

Key: g minor   Cadence: Half

Cadence: Authentic

3. Provide an answer (the term in the correct language) for each of the following.

    a) A German Term meaning "very": _sehr_

10 b) A French Term meaning "fast": _vite_

    c) An Italian Term meaning "with mute": _con sordino_

    d) A German Term meaning "moving": _bewegt_

    e) A French Term meaning "slowly": _lentement_

    f) An Italian Term meaning "broadly": _largamente_

    g) A French Term meaning "yield; hold the tempo back": _cédez_

    h) An Italian Term meaning "the same tempo": _l'istesso tempo_

    i) A term for a bowed string instrument that means "resume bowing after a *pizzicato* passage": _arco_

    j) A term for a bowed string instrument that means "pluck the string instead of bowing": _pizzicato_

4. a) Write the following harmonic intervals below each of the given notes.

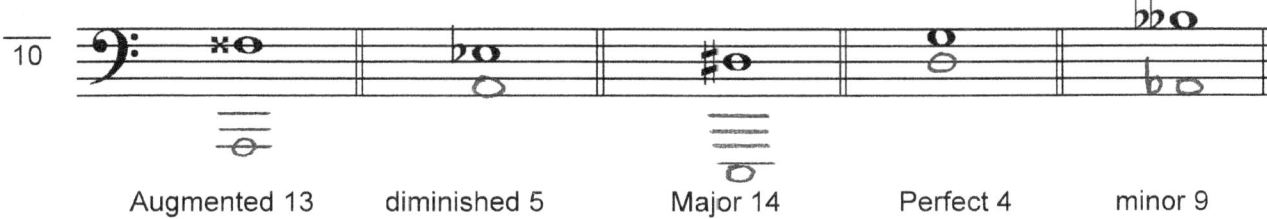

Augmented 13   diminished 5   Major 14   Perfect 4   minor 9

    b) Invert the above intervals in the same clef. Name the inversions.

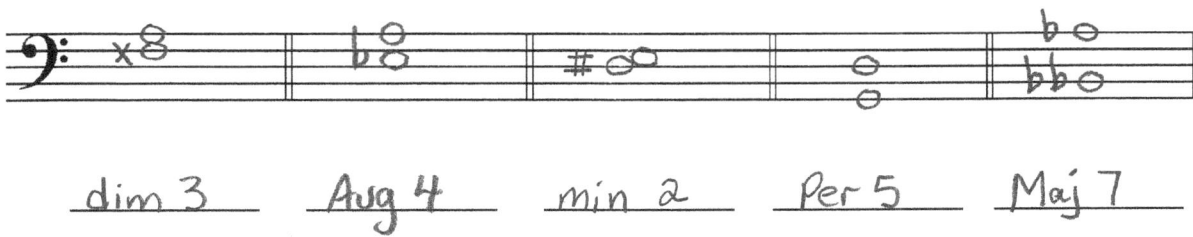

dim 3   Aug 4   min 2   Per 5   Maj 7

5. Match each description in the left column with the correct chord in the right column.

10   __d__   vii°7 in c♯ minor   a)

      __e__   Polychord   b)

      __f__   Submediant Triad in E Major   c)

      __j__   V$^6_5$ in E Major   d)

      __h__   Quartal Chord   e)

      __g__   V$^4_3$ in c♯ minor   f)

      __c__   Cluster Chord   g)

      __i__   G♯m/B   h)

      __a__   E+/B♯   i)

      __b__   Submediant Triad in c♯ minor   j)

Ultimate Music Theory
LEVEL 8 Supplemental Exam #8
Use with Advanced Exam Set 2 - Exam #4

Total Score: _____
50

1. Provide the answer for any 10 (TEN) of the following.

   10

   a) Name one important Renaissance Composer: _Josquin des Prez_

   b) Name one important Medieval Composer: _Hildegard von Bingen_

   c) Name the texture when all voices have the same rhythmic pattern, creating a blocked chordal style: _Homorhythmic texture_

   d) Name the texture of a single unaccompanied melody: _Monophonic texture_

   e) Name a Renaissance Secular Polyphonic Vocal Genre: _Frottola_

   f) Name the term for music performed without accompaniment (literally meaning "for the chapel"): _A cappella_

   g) Name the title of one Medieval Era vocal work: _Ordo Virtutum_

   h) Name the term when the music mirrors the text/words: _Word Painting_

   i) Name one instrumental ensemble associated with "Java" ("Javanese") Music: _Gamelan_

   j) Name the Medieval Genre using a monophonic modal melody with unmeasured rhythm and Latin text: _Plainchant_

   k) Name the multi-stringed plucked instrument with frets that is associated with the music of India: _Sitar_

   l) Name the Medieval Genre that combined drama and music to teach appropriate/desirable behavior: _Morality play_

   m) Name the Contrapuntal Texture that combines 2 or more independent melodic lines: _Polyphonic texture_

2. In the given clef, write the following Seventh Chords. Use a Key Signature. Use half notes.

   10

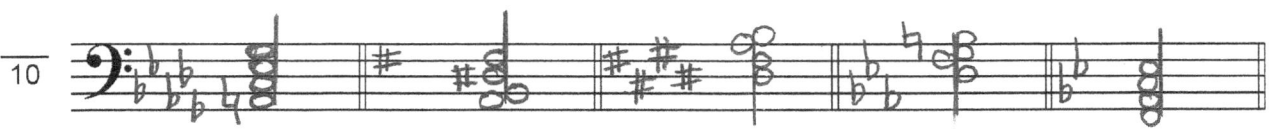

   vii°7 of b♭ minor   V$_2^4$ of e minor   V$_5^6$ of E Major   V$_3^4$ of c minor   V^7 of B♭ Major

3. For the following Melodic Opening:

    a) Name the key of the melody.

    b) Write the Time Signature directly on the music.

10 c) Complete the given melodic opening to create a Question Phrase. End on an unstable scale degree. (There will be more than one correct answer.)

    d) Compose an Answer Phrase to create a Contrasting Period. End on a stable scale degree. (There will be more than one correct answer.)

    e) Draw a phrase mark (slur) over each phrase.

Key: _F# Major_

4. Circle whether the rests in each measure are CORRECT or INCORRECT.

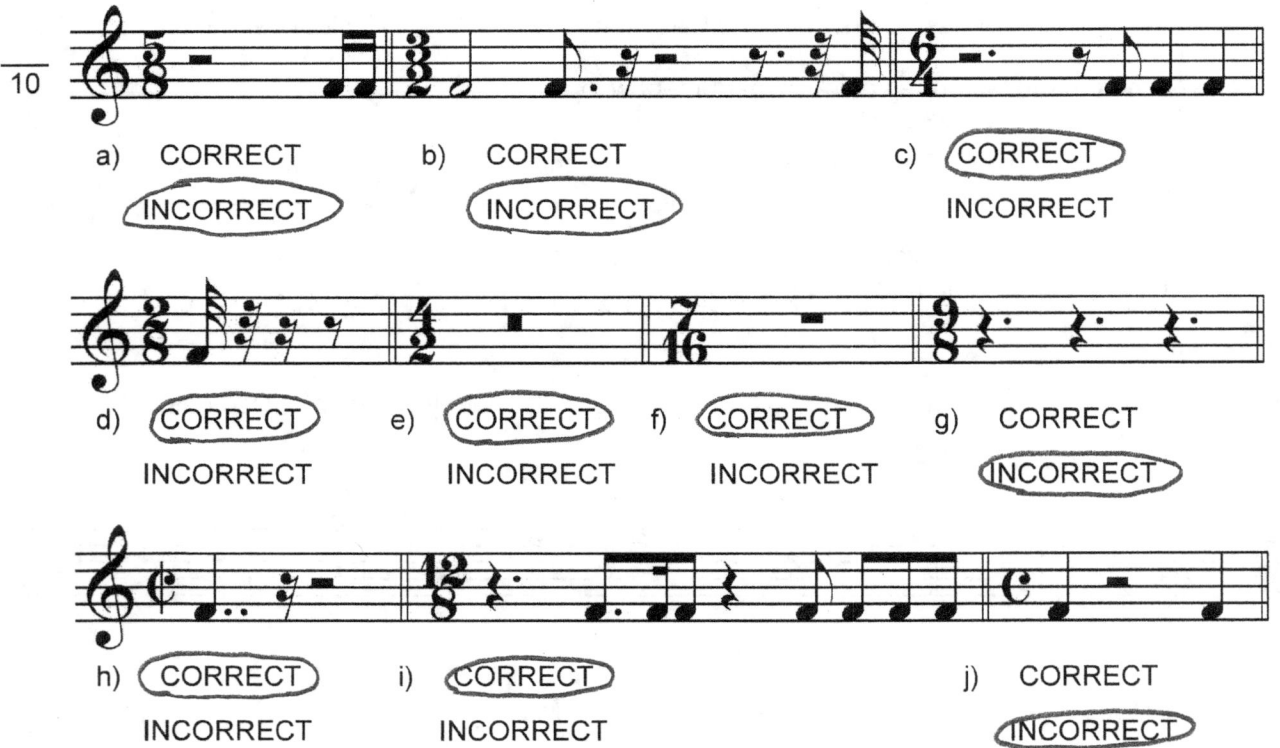

10

  a)   CORRECT   b)   CORRECT   c) (CORRECT)

     (INCORRECT)   (INCORRECT)   INCORRECT

  d) (CORRECT)   e) (CORRECT)   f) (CORRECT)   g) CORRECT

     INCORRECT   INCORRECT   INCORRECT   (INCORRECT)

  h) (CORRECT)   i) (CORRECT)   j) CORRECT

     INCORRECT   INCORRECT   (INCORRECT)

Ultimate Music Theory
LEVEL 8 Supplemental Exam #8

5. Write the following cadences. Use a Key Signature and any necessary accidentals. Use the correct note values (observing any given rests). There will be more than one correct answer for each Cadence.

10
a) Plagal (IV - I) Cadence in E Major written in Chorale Style.
b) Authentic (V - i) Cadence in b minor written in Keyboard Style.
c) Half (iv - V) Cadence in d minor written in Chorale Style.

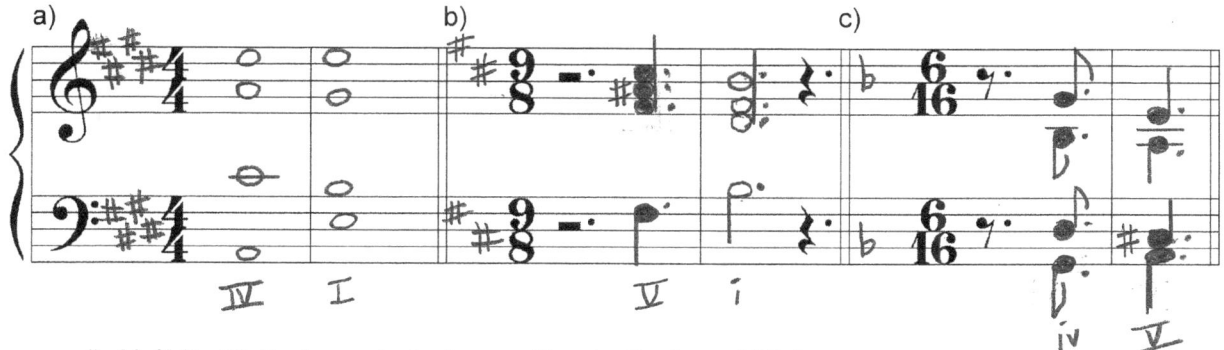

d) Half (i - V) Cadence in f minor written in Keyboard Style.
e) Authentic (V - I) Cadence in G Major written in Keyboard Style.
f) Plagal (iv - i) Cadence in c minor written in Chorale Style.

g) Plagal (IV - I) Cadence in E♭ Major written in Chorale Style.
h) Half (I - V) Cadence F Major written in Chorale Style.
i) Authentic (V - i) Cadence in g minor written in Keyboard Style.
j) Half (IV - V) Cadence in D Major written in Keyboard Style.

1. a) Write the following Solid (Blocked) Triads or Chords. Use a Key Signature and any necessary accidentals. Use whole notes. Write the Root/Quality Chord Symbol above and the Functional Chord Symbol below.

10

Dominant 7th Chord of f♯ minor, 3rd inversion.

Root/Quality Chord Symbol: $C\sharp^7/B$

Functional Chord Symbol: $V\frac{4}{2}$

Diminished 7th Chord of f minor, root position.

Root/Quality Chord Symbol: E^{o7}

Functional Chord Symbol: vii^{o7}

Subtonic Triad of g♯ minor, 2nd inversion.

Root/Quality Chord Symbol: $F\sharp/C\sharp$

Functional Chord Symbol: $VII\frac{6}{4}$

Mediant Triad of D♭ Major, 1st inversion.

Root/Quality Chord Symbol: $Fm/A\flat$

Functional Chord Symbol: $iii\frac{6}{3}$

Submediant Triad of c♯ minor, 2nd inversion.

Root/Quality Chord Symbol: A/E

Functional Chord Symbol: $VI\frac{6}{4}$

Leading Note Triad of B Major, 1st inversion.

Root/Quality Chord Symbol: $A\sharp^o/C\sharp$

Functional Chord Symbol: $vii^{o}\frac{6}{3}$

b) For each of the following Dominant Seventh Chords, name the Key. Write the Root/Quality Chord Symbol above and the Functional Chord Symbol below.

Root/Quality Chord Symbol: $G\flat^7/B\flat$ $D\sharp^7/A\sharp$ $B\flat^7/A\flat$ B^7

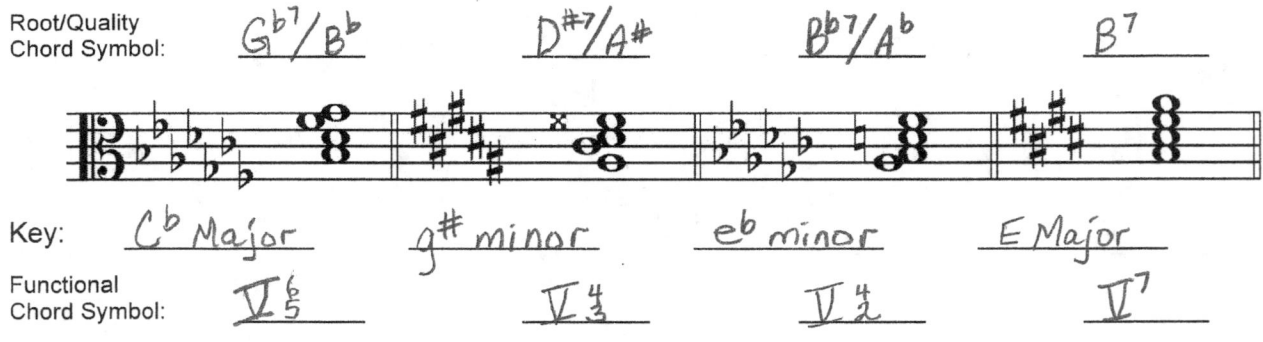

Key: $C\flat$ Major $g\sharp$ minor $e\flat$ minor E Major

Functional Chord Symbol: $V\frac{6}{5}$ $V\frac{4}{3}$ $V\frac{4}{2}$ V^7

2.   a) For each of the following Cadences:
     i) Name the key.
     ii) Name the type of cadence (Authentic, Plagal or Half).

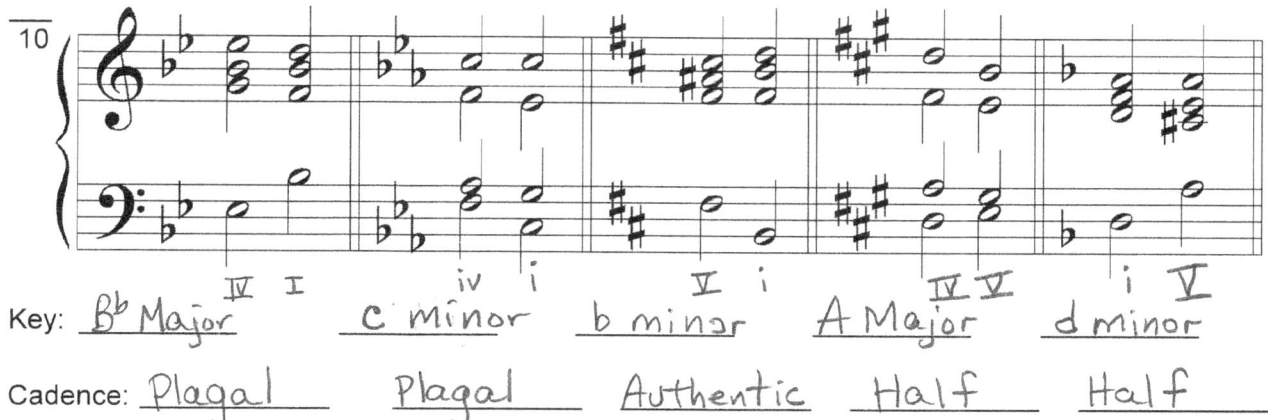

Key: Bb Major   c minor   b minor   A Major   d minor

Cadence: Plagal   Plagal   Authentic   Half   Half

b) For each of the following melodies:
   iii) Name the key.
   iv) Write a cadence in Keyboard Style below the bracketed notes.
   v) Label the chords using Functional Chord Symbols.
   vi) Name the type of cadence as Authentic, Half or Plagal.

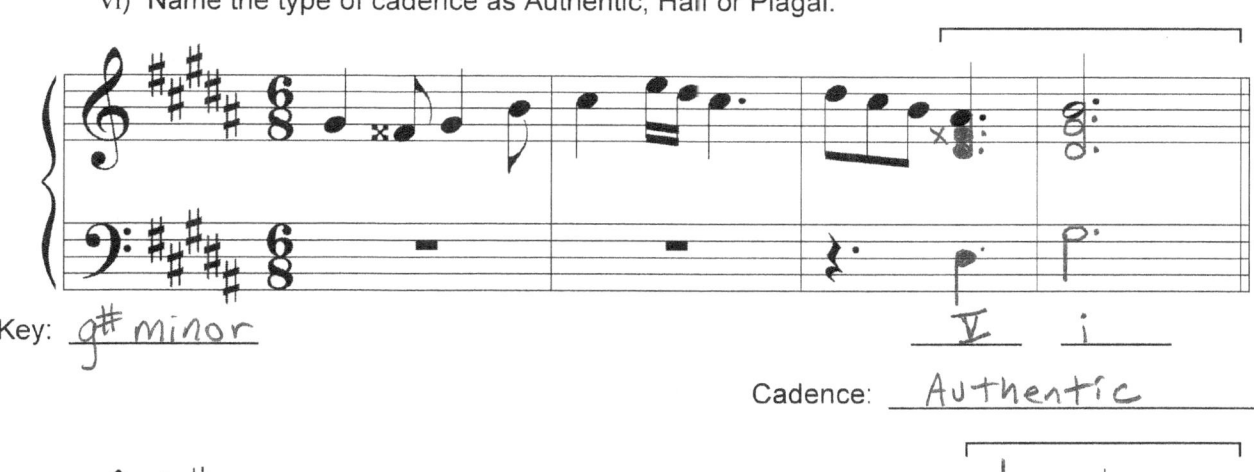

Key: g# minor

Cadence: Authentic

Key: B Major

Cadence: Plagal

3. a) Write the scale, ascending and descending. Use accidentals. Use whole notes.
    Identify the name of the Mode (the Modal Scale) for each of the scales.

____
10

i) E flat Major Scale, from Subdominant to Subdominant. Mode: __Lydian__.

ii) F sharp Major Scale, from Supertonic to Supertonic. Mode: __Dorian__.

iii) B flat Major Scale, from Dominant to Dominant. Mode: __Mixolydian__.

b) Write the minor Pentatonic Scale starting on F. Use any standard version. Use whole notes.

c) Write the Octatonic Scale starting on F. Use any standard version. Use whole notes.
   one possible answer

d) Write the Blues Scale starting on F. Use any standard version. Use whole notes.
   One possible answer

e) Write the Whole-Tone Scale starting on F. Use any standard version. Use whole notes.
   one possible answer

4. a) Add rests below the brackets to complete each of the following measures.

b) Add the correct Time Signature below each bracket to complete the following rhythms.

c) Add bar lines to complete the following rhythms.

5.　a) Write the Melodic Interval below the given note. Use whole notes.

10

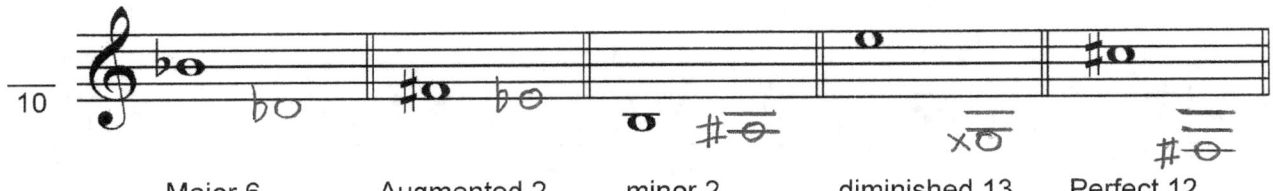

　　Major 6　　　Augmented 2　　　minor 2　　　diminished 13　　　Perfect 12

　　b) Write the Melodic Interval above the given note. Use whole notes.

　　Augmented 4　　diminished 14　　　Perfect 8　　　Major 10　　　Augmented 1

　　c) Name the following intervals.

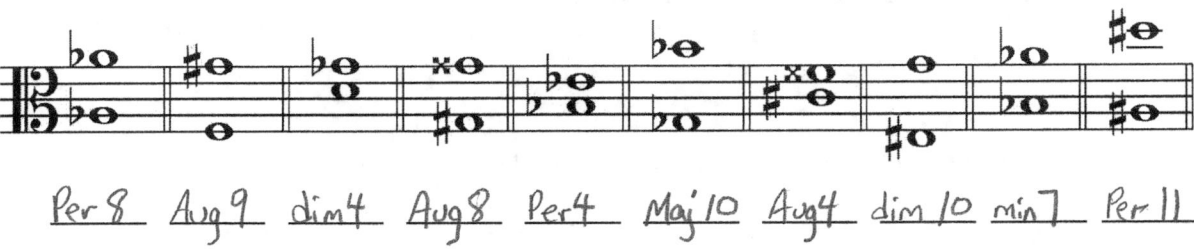

Per 8　Aug 9　dim 4　Aug 8　Per 4　Maj 10　Aug 4　dim 10　min 7　Per 11

6.　For each of the following Chords:
　　a) Name the Chord Type as a Triad, Dominant Seventh or Quartal.
　　b) Rewrite each Chord in the specified type of Open Score.

10

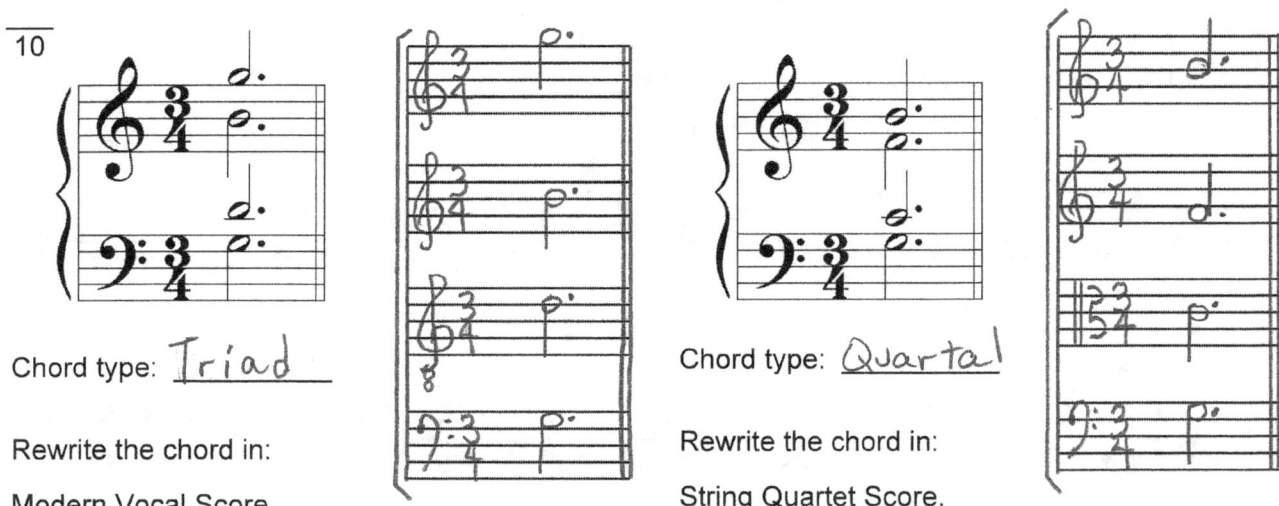

Chord type: Triad

Rewrite the chord in:

Modern Vocal Score.

Chord type: Quartal

Rewrite the chord in:

String Quartet Score.

7. a) The following passage is written for Trumpet in B flat. Name the key in which it is written.
    Transpose it to Concert Pitch. Use the correct Key Signature. Name the new key.

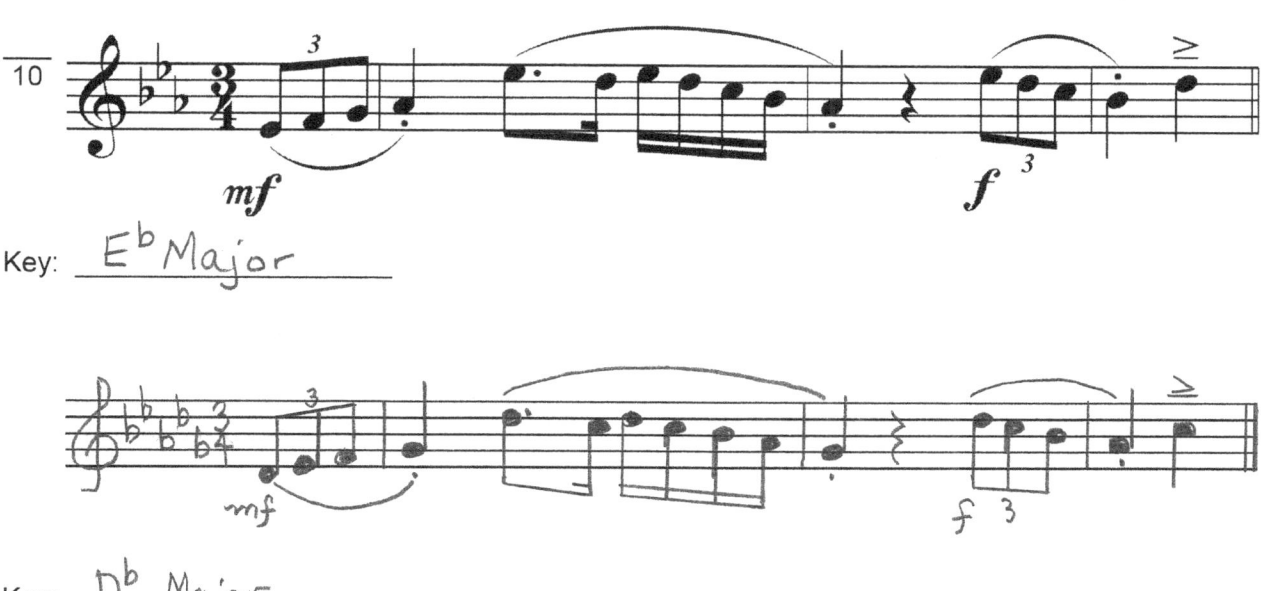

Key: ___E♭ Major___

Key: ___D♭ Major___

b) Name the Key of the following melody. Transpose it down into the key of f sharp minor using
the correct Key Signature. Name the Interval of Transposition.

Key: ___C minor___

Interval of Transposition: ___dim 5___

8. a) For the following Melodic Opening:

    i) Name the key of the melody.
    ii) Complete the given melodic opening to create a Question Phrase. End on an unstable scale degree. Name the Cadence. (There will be more than one correct answer.)
    iii) Compose an Answer Phrase to create a **Contrasting Period**. End on a stable scale degree. Name the Cadence. (There will be more than one correct answer.)
    iv) Draw a phrase mark (slur) over each phrase.

$\overline{10}$

Key: __f# minor__   Cadence: __Half__

Cadence: __Authentic__

b) For each of the following melodies:

    i) Name the key of the melody.
    ii) Write the Functional Chord Symbols on the lines below each measure.
    iii) Circle the non-chord tones and label each as **pt** or **nt**.

Key: __Db Major__

Key: __g# minor__

9. a) Provide the definition for FIVE (5) of the following terms. *(All answers are given)*
only 5 are required

i) *sforzando*: a sudden strong accent of a single note *or chord*

10

ii) *con sordino*: with mute

iii) *l'istesso tempo*: the same tempo

iv) *comodo*: at a comfortable, easy tempo

v) *volti subito*: turn the page quickly

vi) *sotto voce*: soft, subdued, under the breath

vii) *morendo*: dying, fading away

viii) *martellato*: strongly accented, hammered

b) Choose the correct description to identify any FIVE (5) of the following statements.

i) A source of melodic improvisation in Indian Classical Music:
☑ - Raga. ☐ - Sitar.

ii) An anonymous 13th century round:
☐ - El grillo. ☑ - Sumer Is Icumen In.

iii) A morality play by Hildegard von Bingen:
☑ - Ordo Virtutum. ☐ - Gamelan Prawa.

iv) A frottola by Josquin des Prez:
☐ - Evening Raga. ☑ - El grillo.

v) A single voice texture:
☐ - Homophonic. ☑ - Monophonic.

vi) A Javenese Ensemble consisting mainly of metallophones:
☑ - Gamelan. ☐ - Sitar.

vii) A recurring rhythmic or melodic pattern:
☑ - Ostinato. ☐ - Plainchant.

viii) A motion that occurs when two voices move in the opposite direction:
☐ - Oblique. ☑ - Contrary.

10. Analyze the final excerpt from Ultimate Music Theory Student Olivia Allen's Sonatina in C Major by answering the questions below.

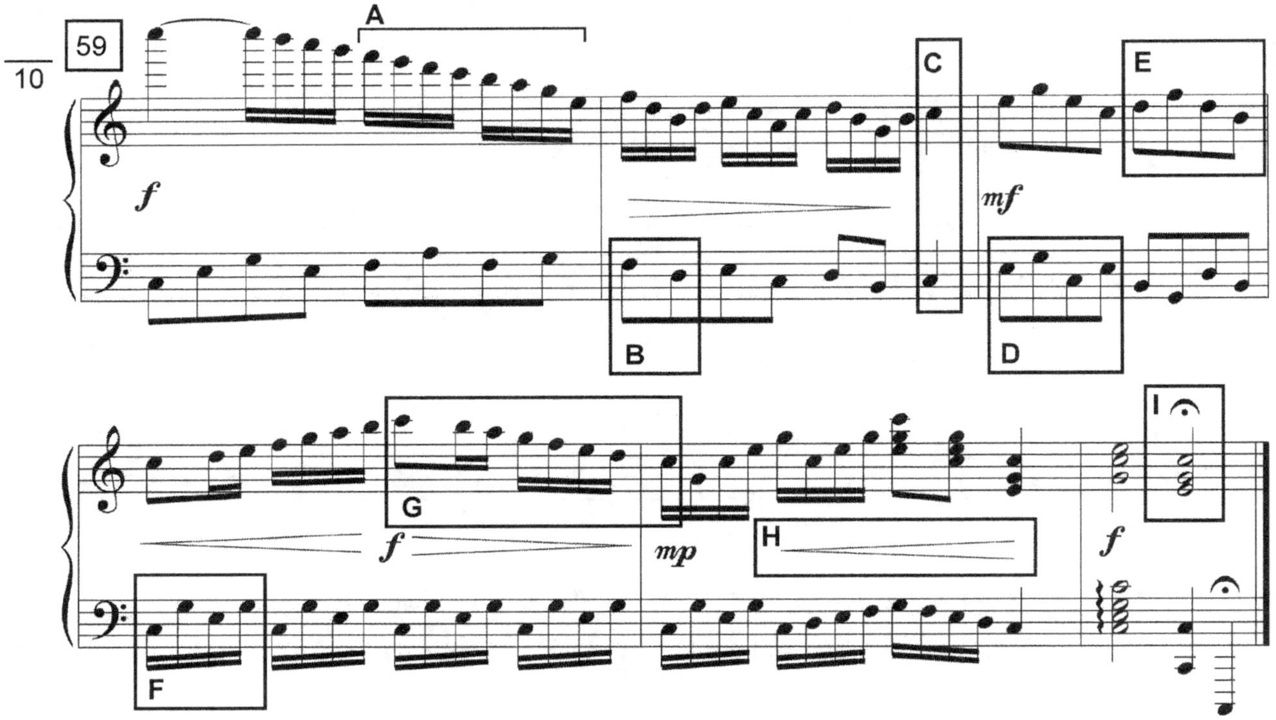

a) Identify the note names below **A**: __F__, __E__, __D__, __C__, __B__, __A__, __G__, __E__.

b) For the Interval at **B**, identify the type as: (Melodic) or Harmonic.

c) For the Interval at **C**, identify the type as: Simple or (Compound.)

d) Identify the interval at letter **B**. __min 3__. Identify the interval at letter **C**. __Per 15__.

e) For the Triad at **D**, identify: Root: __C__ Quality: __Major__ Position: __root pos__.

f) For the Triad at **E**, identify: Root: __B__ Quality: __diminished__ Position: __root pos__.

g) Identify the number of times the Ostinato Pattern at **F** is played in Measure 62: __4__.

h) Identify the Scale at **G**: __C Major__. Identify the direction: __descending__.

i) Identify and Explain the sign at **H**: __Crescendo, becoming louder__

j) Identify and Explain the sign at **I**: __fermata pause, hold longer than__
__its written value.__

TOP 10 Ultimate Music Theory Tips
To Score 100% on Exams

Tip #1: Students should complete at least 8 Practice Examinations before writing their Final Exam. LEVEL 8 Exams will have two hours to be completed.

Tip #2: Hold a "Practice Examination" in your studio. Have all students who are writing their Exams come at the same time. They can only bring a ruler, eraser and pencil. Set a Timer. When the timer starts, the examination begins – no talking, no cell phones, no open books!

Tip #3: Pizza Party! On the night before their Examinations, have a "Pizza Party" – Use the Ultimate Music Theory Flashcards App, UMT Whiteboard and UMT Games to review terminology and concepts. Everyone will have fun and everything will be fresh in their minds.

Tip #4: On Exam day, Students should arrive 15 minutes before the start time of their Examination.

Tip #5: If the Student is not given a piece of blank paper to use to write out their UMT Map before beginning their Examination, they should ask for one from the Exam Center Representative. (Have your Student practice asking for a blank piece of paper.)

Tip #6: Remind both Student and Parent that it is the Student's responsibility to bring a mechanical pencil (with extra lead), or 2 - 3 pencils (with a pencil sharpener), eraser and ruler. They cannot bring any items that have "music" on them, so they cannot bring their UMT Rulers.

Tip #7: It is always a good idea to bring a tissue or two, a bottle of water and a couple of hard candies if it is cold/allergy time. Be sure to get plenty of rest the day before the exam.

Tip #8: Complete the exam in order beginning with question 1. Review what your Student can do if they get stuck – if their brain goes blank on a question. One suggestion would be to continue to the next question and then go back later to finish that question.

Tip #9: Remind Students to look at the front AND back of each page to ensure that ALL questions have been answered... and checked... and double checked.

Tip #10: Ultimate Music Theory 100% Club - *The Way to Score Success!* You and your student can become a member of the UMT 100% Club when your student receives a score of 100% on their nationally recognized theory exams including the RCM Theory Examinations.

Go to UltimateMusicTheory.com and complete the UMT 100% Club Form to receive your special 100% Club Certificate & Congratulations!

 **Workbooks, Exams, Answers, Online Courses, App & More!**

A Proven Step-by-Step System to Learn Theory Faster - from Beginner to Advanced.

Innovative techniques designed to develop a complete understanding of music theory, to enhance sight reading, ear training, creativity, composition and musical expression.

All UMT Series have matching Answer Books!

The UMT Rudiments Series - Beginner A, Beginner B, Beginner C, Prep 1, Prep 2, Basic, Intermediate, Advanced & Complete (All-In-One)

♪ 12 Lessons, Review Tests, and a Final Exam to develop confidence
♪ Music Theory Guide & Chart for fast and easy reference of theory concepts
♪ 80 Flashcards for fun drills to dramatically increase retention & comprehension

Rudiments Exam Series - Preparatory, Basic, Intermediate & Advanced

♪ 8 Exams plus UMT Tips on How to Score 100% on Theory Exams

Each Rudiments Workbook correlates to a Supplemental Workbook.

The UMT Supplemental Series - Prep Level, Level 1, Level 2, Level 3, Level 4, Level 5, Level 6, Level 7, Level 8 & Complete (All-In-One) Level

♪ Form & Analysis and Music History - Composers, Eras & Musical Styles
♪ Melody Writing using ICE - Imagine, Compose & Explore
♪ 12 Lessons, Review Tests, Final Exam and 80 Flashcards for quick study

Supplemental Exam Series - Level 5, Level 6, Level 7 & Level 8

♪ 8 Exams to successfully prepare for nationally recognized Theory Exams

UMT Online Courses, Music Theory App & More

♪ UMT Certification Course, Teachers Membership & Elite Educator Program
♪ Ultimate Music Theory App correlates to the Rudiments Workbooks
♪ Free Resources - Teachers Guide, Music Theory Blogs, videos & downloads

Go To: UltimateMusicTheory.com